JOURNEY TO THE TOP

A Journey of Mother and Daughter
Through Dyslexia and Attention Deficit Disorder

Donna L. Holte

FOREWORD BY FARUK S. ABUZZAHAB, SR., MD, PhD

JOURNEY TO THE TOP
by Donna L. Holte
Foreword by Faruk S. Abuzzahab, Sr., MD, PhD

Printed in the United States of America

ISBN 9781624197475

www.xulonpress.com

This book is dedicated…

to all parents and children who struggle with

dyslexia and attention deficit disorder…

and to Sarah's many supporters and prayer warriors!

To God be the glory!

There are two things you can do
When you come to a mountain:
CLIMB IT or **GO AROUND IT**.
The second way is the easiest...
but you miss the view from **the TOP**!
(Author Unknown)

I was climbing up a mountain, headed for the top
My feet started sliding and I almost fell off
I landed on a rocky ledge, suspended in the air
And I cried out in despair...I said,
"Is anybody out there? Anybody there at all?"
Then I saw Him reaching down and I heard Him call:

"Give me your hand, I'll lift you up
Don't be afraid, you just have to trust
I have been there in the place you stand
There's no need to fear, that's why I'm here
Give me your hand"

(Give Me Your Hand[1] by Ray Boltz)

CONTENTS

Foreword

Although at first glance, *Journey to the Top* appears to be autobiographical, Donna L. Holte's account provides valuable lessons that should be engraved in gold and shared with all parents and educators. Ms. Holte's passion, adamant devotion, and faith jump out at the reader between every line as she describes her journey.

Lesson one is that courage and hope lead to positive thinking, which has contributed to crowning Donna's daughter Sarah with success in overcoming her dyslexia and attention deficit disorder (ADD). Studies have indicated that positive attitudes decrease the stress hormone cortisol and indirectly contribute to positive changes in the neurochemistry of the brain, enabling the Brain Derived Nerve Factor (BDNF) to enrich and stimulate growth of our brain cells.

The second lesson from Donna L. Holte's book is for parents and educators to mount a national plea to have the methods for dyslexics developed by Landmark College in Putney, Vermont, to be adopted universally at all levels of education from pre-kindergarten to colleges of higher learning. This will reverse the present tendency that children with dyslexia and attention deficit disorder (ADD) are being ignored, marginalized, and stigmatized.

The third lesson evolves from Sarah's positive response to medication. Positron Emission Tomography (PET) scanning of the brains of patients with attention deficit disorder (ADD) has demonstrated neurotransmitter disturbances were corrected after treatment with medications. In spite of this convincing scientific evidence, there is a fear of administering medication to children and adolescents. Withholding appropriate medications for attention deficit disorder (ADD) is equivalent to withholding life-saving antibiotics to a person with pneumonia or not giving insulin to patients with juvenile diabetes.

The fourth and final lesson is that children suffering from dyslexia and attention deficit disorder (ADD) are children of God. They are gifted in being able to think outside the confinement of the box of the establishment. They tend to be adventurous and very creative. They were not meant to just sit and dot the i's and cross the t's. The success of Sarah, the "Princess," after all her struggles, is a living example that the arduous journey to the top of the mountain afforded her a magnificent view of the world around her.

This journey can now be pursued by everybody who has dyslexia and attention deficit disorder (ADD). Watch out, Sarah, for the thundering stampede of others with dyslexia

and attention deficit disorder (ADD) following your steps
to the top of the mountain!

Faruk S. Abuzzahab, Sr., MD, PhD
Adjunct Professor, Psychiatry, Pharmacology, Family
Practice, and Community Health; University of Minnesota

Distinguished Life Fellow; American Psychiatric
Association

Emeritus Fellow; American College of Clinical
Pharmacology

Emeritus Fellow; Collegium Internationale
Neuro-Psychopharmacologicum

Emeritus Member; American Society of Pharmacology and
Experimental Therapeutics

Preface

"Don't look for the Victory—look for Me,
and I will bring the Victory!"[2] Frances J. Roberts

his book was "birthed" after our daughter, Sarah, became engaged. Her fiancé certainly knew our daughter well — but he couldn't possibly have learned, in their courtship days, everything *I* knew about her. So, I decided to put together an album/scrapbook for him titled "The Sarah *I* Know." This album started out with baby pictures and a copy of the name plaque that is up in our home:

SARAH

GOD'S PRINCESS

. . . The Lord will arise upon you,
and His glory will be seen upon you.

--Isaiah 60:2

Then I included the other plaque in our home, which reads:

For this child I prayed; and the Lord has granted me my petition which I made to Him. Therefore I have lent [her] to the Lord. As long as [she] lives, [she] is lent to the Lord. 1 Samuel 1:27–28

This was followed with pages of pictures titled:

THE SARAH I KNOW...
...Has tons of friends!
...Loves parties!
...Loves shopping!
...Is "fun"!
...Loves to do...well...everything!
...Is loving!
...Loves family!
...Is caring!
...Is very creative!
...Is a survivor...my hero!
...Is a child of God!
...Is being married...
    Love her!
    Protect her!
    Live life together!
    Have fun together!
    Grow spiritually with her!
    Worship together!
    As two cherished children of God!

It was fun putting this together and reliving many memories—both fun as well as painful memories. And it was during this process of reliving that I kept thinking: *But there is so much more to tell. I need to tell the story of the PAIN as well, during all of those fun years—but only to share the VICTORY through faith as the final outcome of the pain in Sarah's life.* The pain was living with dyslexia and attention deficit disorder (ADD)[3]; but the victory came only as we turned her life over to our God and Savior!

So, after we celebrated Sarah's wedding and she began her married life, I was encouraged to write this book—not only for her husband, but also for others who share this pain and hopefully can share in the victory too!

I needed to share how powerfully God touched Sarah's life during those painful years and, in turn, my life as well. All through those years I saw the "special touches" of God—the small miracles—even though no touch of God is small! I'm not at all sure that Sarah always recognized those "God-touches" at the time, but she most certainly did in her later years. This book is a witness to the faithfulness of God and to the victory that He will bring when we follow His command to TRUST HIM, to leave our lives in His hands according to *His will, not ours*, and to praise Him continually! I would *never* have dared to ask or hope for—or even *dream* of hoping for—how God, in His time and according to His will, answered our prayers for Sarah's life.

ACKNOWLEDGMENTS

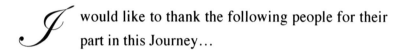

$\mathcal{I}$ would like to thank the following people for their part in this Journey…

- *Gail Swenson* – for editing the first draft of this book. Gail, you not only did the editing, but you encouraged me to keep going!
- *Terri Bailey* – for editing, typing, and formatting the final draft. Thank you for hanging in there with me all the way. I am thrilled with your expertise in this area!
- *Hulda Gieschen* – for drawing the mountain for the front cover. You could draw this mountain because you were with me as I was writing this story and knew what "climbing a mountain" meant for Sarah.
- *Dr. Abuzzahab* – for his exceptional medical expertise and for offering to write the forward to this book. You know what you mean to Sarah and our family and we thank you deeply for that.
- *My granddaughter, Megan Riggott* – what can I say? Without you, this book would not have been written. The time and dedication you have put into this process

is overwhelming and I love you dearly for it. You have been my inspiration, my encourager, and my expertise in everything it takes to write a book!

- *Sarah's many friends* – you know who you are, but you may not know how invaluable your love, friendship, and support has been to her and to me!

- *Minnehaha Academy, Elayne, and Cookie* – for always being there at just the right times.

- *Landmark College, Carolyn Olivier, John Bagge, and Diane Wood* – for being there as supporters, mentors, and friends for Sarah.

- *Trudy Winstead* – for allowing me to share your article, "Thy Name is Courage." I looked to this powerful article for encouragement during many years of struggling.

- *Sue Martindale* – for re-creating many of the graphics at the last minute, not to mention late at night!

- *Karla at Xulon Press* – for mentoring me in publishing my first book and for your patience with my questions.

- *Lorna, my deceased friend, and Betty* – my prayer warriors through most of this journey – and all my other friends and family who have been praying.

- *My husband, Rich* – for all the love, caring, and bringing meals to my office while I was writing this book.

- *My daughters, Kathy and Debby* – for all the many years of your love and support for Sarah while she was struggling.

- *Sarah and Larry* – thank you for letting me share

"our" journey. Your love during this process has been incredible!

- *My Lord and Savior* – for being with Sarah from the moment of her birth and for walking with her each day…thank You! You are my Lord and Savior and You have given me Your peace and strength and equipped me with Your inspired words for this book!

Prologue

"THE STORY OF A JOURNEY...TO THE TOP!"

Journey of Mother and Daughter, with God, through dyslexia and attention deficit disorder (ADD).

A Journey of...

...a Mother who trusted in her God...a God who said, *Seek ye first the Kingdom of God and all else will be added unto you*...a Daughter who listened and began her climb.

...a Mother who trusted...a God who said, *I know the plans I have for you; plans for good and not for evil*...a Daughter who listened and kept her eyes upon Jesus.

...a Mother who trusted...a God who said, *I give My best to those who leave the choice to Me*...a Daughter who listened and continued her climb.

...a Mother who trusted...a God who said, *Take My hand this day and walk with Me*...a Daughter who listened and put her hand in His each day.

...a Mother who trusted...a God who said, *See, I will not forget you; I have carved you on the palm of My hand*...a Daughter who listened and rested in the palm of His hand.

...a Mother who trusted...a God who said, *The battle belongs to Me*...a Daughter who listened and kept her eyes upon the Lord.

...a Mother who trusted...a God who said, *Trust My silence*... a Daughter who listened and, in trust, climbed without questioning.

...a Mother who trusted...a God who said, *My timing is best*...a Daughter who listened and waited on God.

...a Mother who trusted...a God who said, *My plans are unshakable*...a Daughter who listened and climbed with confidence.

...a Mother who trusted...a God who said, *I will keep you in perfect peace*...a Daughter who listened and rested in peace as she climbed.

...a Mother who trusted...a God who said, *Great is My faithfulness*...a Daughter who listened, trusted in His faithfulness, and made it...**to the TOP!**

Introduction

I looked at my watch. It was now 7 a.m. on a school morning, and I still did not hear any rustling in Sarah's bedroom above me. I tried so hard to let her be responsible for setting her own alarm clock and getting up in the morning—after all, she was in the eighth grade. But now it was time: time for me to intervene and wake her up so she would not be late for school. I dreaded this, and it was with trepidation that I climbed the stairs to the bedroom on the left. *Please God, be with me*, I whispered in my heart.

I opened the door a crack and looked into her messy bedroom. I saw a huge lump under her pink flowered quilt and knew she was again trying to avoid facing the world; I would often find her buried under all the covers. I walked in, trying to avoid stepping on the clothes all over the floor, and then sat quietly on the bed and pulled back the quilt ever so gently. I brushed her hair away from her face, gently rubbed her back, gave her a quick kiss, and whispered, "Honey, it is time to get up." She did not move for a time, but then as I gently nudged her, she cried, "Go away! I don't feel good. I can't go to school today." This always set me back a bit, but it had happened before. "Honey, you have to go to school today; you missed school yesterday. And remember, after you got up yesterday you felt fine."

Then it came—something that I *had not* heard before. Sarah suddenly threw off the covers and yelled at me passionately, "But you don't understand! I was awake all night crying and hoping to wake up from this nightmare: this nightmare called 'She has a learning disability!'" Sarah had been diagnosed as having both dyslexia and attention deficit disorder (ADD). My heart was breaking, and with tears in my eyes I looked up and saw the plaque on the wall above her bed, the plaque I had put up just the week before:

KEEP YOUR EYES UPON JESUS

I knew that at that moment I had to do just that: KEEP MY EYES ON JESUS!

Sarah and mom's journey with this nightmare called "She has a learning disability" had begun long before. And, as I was reminded once again that morning, this journey of ours had been most importantly a faith journey!

My own faith journey began when I was a child. I was baptized, confirmed, and grew up in a Christian family.

Throughout my childhood and early young adulthood, I remember my father always having family devotions at the dinner table and nighttime prayers together before going to bed. But it was during my years at a Christian college that I renewed my faith in a meaningful way. I remember many quiet times alone kneeling in the college chapel in the evening. For the first time, my faith became a personal relationship with God.

But then, in the years following—with a new job, a new marriage, and becoming the new mother of two adopted daughters—my faith took a backseat. I'm not sure I even realized it; I was just too preoccupied and concerned about meeting the demands of each new day. And during those years of understandable stress, when I should have been turning to my faith and my God for His strength and peace, I failed myself and my God. I tried to do it all alone! It was only after I became mother of a new infant—Sarah, a child of God given to me to love and guide and care for in this earthly life—did God reveal to me that I could *not* do it all alone!

Sarah struggled day in and day out, many nights crying out to God all night long to be able to wake up from this nightmare—this nightmare called "She has a learning disability." And along with the struggle of her learning disabilities came a myriad of other trials. Talking with God and listening to Him speak to me during my devotional time in His Word gave me the peace and strength and assurance that all would be well with Sarah, His child—if I would only leave her in **His Hands**, rely on **His Faithfulness**, be patient during **His Silence**, and wait for **His Timing**.

I spent many hours searching for information and counseling on dyslexia and attention deficit disorder (ADD). But along with this, and most importantly of all, I spent many, many hours on my knees in prayer asking God for His direction and guidance and praising Him, even in the midst of our many trials.

And in God's time, Sarah went on to graduate from college, worked as a regional representative for the first college in the world exclusively for students with learning difficulties, married a wonderful Christian man, and has an amazing life filled with God and His overwhelming blessings! This is the story of our "journey" to that end—the journey of a mother and daughter, with God, through dyslexia and attention deficit disorder (ADD).

Chapter 1

"IT'S A GIRL!"

*"You saw me before I was born and scheduled each day of
my life before I began to breathe."* Psalms 139:16

anuary 8, 1968…it was 5:30 p.m. and I had just left
the dinner table to sit on the sofa in the adjacent
family room while my family finished dinner. I thought to
myself, *It must be almost time.* I was right! Just six hours
later, the doctor at Fairview Southdale Hospital handed me
our new six-pound five-ounce daughter. If you have never
been a mother, you would not know the overwhelming emotion of being handed this gift from God. I can almost feel the
intensity of that emotion to this day.

But let me start from the beginning of this mother and
daughter's incredible journey with God. The journey actu-
ally began for me personally in 1962, after I graduated from
Wartburg College in Waverly, Iowa. I had recently moved to
Minneapolis, Minnesota, to begin my new job as Director of
Education at Bethlehem Lutheran Church.

I began my new job under the direction of Pastor Bill,

Youth Pastor at Bethlehem Lutheran Church. He was my advisor, mentor, friend...and eventually my "match-maker." Along with my duties in education, I was also involved in the youth program and became a Hi-League counselor. As Youth Pastor, Pastor Bill (as we lovingly called him) ministered to all unmarried young people.

At that time it was harder to form a group of post-college singles than it was of high school students. So, Pastor Bill developed a unique way of reaching out to this age group. He called it his "blind-date ministry." As he moved among the congregation or wherever else life took him, he was deeply interested in the young people he encountered and knew what he was looking for in each of them. His constant companion was his little black book. I remember him returning one afternoon from a trip downtown to buy a tie. He came into my office, pulled out his little black book, and proceeded to tell me about the name he had just added. He was very impressed with the clerk who had sold him the tie and had asked if he would be interested in a blind date with a Christian girl. He took down the young man's name and telephone number and told him he would call him at a later date. In this way, Pastor Bill compiled his list for his blind-date ministry.

About three times a year, Pastor Bill arranged dinner at the church for a group of about eight couples on blind dates. After Pastor Bill chose a girl for a particular young man, it became the responsibility of the guy to call her, arrange the "date," and pick her up. The group would meet for dinner and informal conversation, listen to a brief message from Pastor Bill, and then be off to a movie or a play. This was his unique ministry to post-college-age young people. And he had a number of successes resulting in long-term commitments!

It was early in January 1964 when Pastor Bill again came into my office. But, instead of pulling out his little black book, he gave me a big smile and told me he had somebody special in mind for *me* for his next blind-date dinner. He was very excited, but also very cautious. He wanted to be sure that this was something I wanted as well. He had gotten to know Rich, a young man from our congregation, who was a homebuilder upon whom Pastor Bill had called to do some work in his own home. Rich was thirty-seven years old and a widower with two young daughters, aged ten and thirteen. They had lost their mother when they were two and five years old. Rich, with the help of his extended family, had been raising them since then. Pastor Bill was very excited for me to meet him. So it was...we would meet at the next blind-date dinner on January 24.

Now, anyone who knew Rich at this time knew that he was a little shy and not very outgoing. He did, however, know who I was. His daughters were in our Sunday school, so of course he knew who the Director of Education was. So, he agreed...he would go on a blind date with me. He called me for the date, and we had a very good time at the dinner and play. Now, because Rich was shy, that could have been the end of it. But he did call me after the blind date to ask if I could go for dinner the following Friday night. *Oh no,*

I thought, *I have a meeting at church that night. Now what do I do?* I really wanted to go out with him again, but "nice" girls in my day did not do what I was thinking of doing. But, I did it anyway! I said, "I can't go out on Friday night, but I *can* on Saturday night." Reflecting on my decision years later, knowing Rich as I do now, I am convinced that God prompted me to be that bold. If I had turned Rich down for Friday night, he would *never* have asked again.

Thank you...thank you...thank you, God!

In October of that year, I sent the following note to all my friends and family:

I'VE BEEN ACCEPTED!

I'm leaving my job at Bethlehem for an exciting new position!

My new job begins: May 1 at 4:00 p.m.

Responsibilities: Wife to a handsome husband and mother to two beautiful daughters.

Salary: Room and board on Sheridan Avenue.

Benefits: All the love and affection from three treasured people!

Tenure: A Lifetime!

Rich and I were married on May 1, 1965, and on that day I became a new wife and the mother of two very special daughters, Kathy and Debby. Rich and I spent the month of May in Florida on a honeymoon before coming home to Minneapolis to begin bonding as a family. A year later I officially adopted the girls, but to this day I have never considered them "adopted"—they are truly my own dear daughters!

Rich's gifts as a homebuilder came to him naturally. He comes from a family of builders, including his father and two brothers. He was working with a brother when we met, but began working the next year as foreman for another builder. He kept this position until his retirement, building many homes in Minneapolis and the western suburbs. During the September following our honeymoon, we moved into our first (and only) home, which Rich had built for us in South Minneapolis. It was in this home and within this family that the "Journey" began...the journey of a mother and her daughter with God through dyslexia and attention deficit disorder (ADD).

Sarah Elizabeth was born into our family: Mom, Dad, and two sisters, ages thirteen and sixteen. Kathy and Debby had been such brave and special girls since their biological mother died eleven years earlier. So it was on that late night of January 8, 1968, God placed in my hands another child to watch over and care for. Because Sarah was my first biological child, I was a little nervous on the first night home with an infant. I had done some babysitting, but never for a newborn! I'm sure I did not sleep much that first night, even though she only woke up twice. For just a few nights, the new white bassinet that I had spent so much time preparing for her was right beside our bed. But soon we moved her into the nursery, and she and I did just fine.

I remember so clearly and can picture so vividly the night I first gave my daughter to God and laid her in His hands. She was about two weeks old and had a cold. Even though I was told this was not unusual and was nothing to worry about, I *was* worried! I held her in my arms for most of the night, rocking her in the small blue rocker in the nursery. I looked down at her, so tiny and fragile, and prayed, *God, please keep her safe and, in return, I give her to you. She will be Your child from this day forward.* It didn't take long for me to realize that she was *already* God's child, and all that I really had to do was release her in my heart and then *TRUST HIM!*

Not long after that night, while reading my Bible, I found Hannah's prayer in the book of 1 Samuel; her prayer has been mine from that day forward:

> *For this child I prayed; and the Lord has granted me my petition which I made to Him. Therefore I have lent [her] to the Lord. As long as [she] lives, [she] is lent to the Lord.* 1 Samuel 1:27–28

I have prayed this prayer on my knees many, many times since that night, reminding myself that Sarah is in God's hands and I need only to trust Him. But, on that night I had no idea what God had in mind for Sarah's life and what truly trusting Him would mean for me and for Sarah. I had no idea what a struggle she would have for so many years to come.

Trusting God was not easy to begin with. Many times I would place Sarah in God's hands, then promptly pull her back again. *God, are you sure this time? Do you really understand what the situation is? Are you sure it is not different this time?* But each time I chose to trust God, it would get easier and He would give me His peace.

Chapter 2

"GO SARAH, GO!"

*"For the Lord watches over all the plans
and paths of godly men."* Psalms 1:6

It started when Sarah was an infant. I can't remember exactly when, but I am sure it was shortly after she was moved to the nursery and continued until she left home to go to college. Each night before I went to bed, I would slip into the nursery or, as she grew older, her bedroom. I would give her a kiss on the forehead and whisper into her ear, "I love you and God loves you!" She was a heavy sleeper, so even when she was older she would never have known I did this, but I know her soul heard this. Later, as she grew, I would kneel at her bed each evening and again each morning after she left for school, sometimes with specific prayer requests, at other times just entrusting her to her Father's capable hands. Leaving her each day in His hands helped carry me through those many days of uncertainty in Sarah's life.

We lived in a wonderful neighborhood in South Minneapolis. By the time Sarah was two years old, there

were a number of families with children her age in the neighborhood. Sarah had neighborhood friends, church friends,
and school friends. Her elementary school was just down
the block from our home. Sarah loved being involved in
many activities, as long as her friends were there. They were
always such a special part of her life. God filled Sarah with
compassion—for friends and family.

I remember so well her first Field Day in first grade.
She was running in the relay. I was there with all the other
moms, and I heard myself shout, "Go Sarah, go!" And then
again, "Go Sarah!" Sarah started out far ahead of the pack,
but—now what was she doing? She had stopped—why?
And then I saw. She held out her hand, waiting for her friend
to catch up with her! I stopped in my tracks, with not another
word, and thought, *Wow! Can a mom ask for anything more?*
Sarah was a caring child who thought not of winning for
herself, but only of her friend! I don't remember who won
the race, but I still remember learning something much more
important that day.

Sarah loved friends. Since her older sisters were now
grown and had moved out of our home, it was important for
her to have these friends. Because the school was just down
the block from our home, many of her friends would stop
in on their way to school and again after school. As I spent
time with her friends, sitting around the table with treats
and chatting, I began to understand something that made an
impact on my life with Sarah. I began to understand that the
way to have a good relationship with my own daughter was

to have a good relationship with my daughter's friends. I truly loved all of her friends, and they included me in their conversations and sharing. If they ever needed a place to be, they always knew they could come to Sarah's house. And they did—often! And we loved it!

Sarah loved being with her friends, and she really loved parties! I'm not sure why I thought this was important, but I began having parties for her when she was two years old, and we had a birthday party every year until she was in high school. Her last high school party was a surprise for her eighteenth birthday with a "This Is Your Life!" theme. Later, I felt one last party was in order—another surprise when she turned thirty years old. As sentimental as I am, I had agonized over getting rid of Sarah's cute childhood clothes and the memories that went along with them. But really, from when she was two years old? So, I came up with the answer: a thirtieth birthday party with a "style show." Sarah, of course, had long moved out of our home. While rummaging through closets full of boxes and hangers, I found dresses upon dresses, as well as many other outfits. Had I really saved all of those clothes? My plan now was to give them all away—after the style show of course! Because the style show would need models from two years old to high-school age, I began calling friends and relatives of all ages. Meanwhile, I found a party room, planned the food, and found a friend to be the style show "moderator."

The surprise went off as planned, and everyone had fun. Because I had a video and many pictures taken during the party, I was able to visually save my sentimental memories of

Sarah in her many clothes. Now I could donate them and get them out of my basement. But could I? Some of the younger children asked to keep the outfits they had modeled, and was I ever happy about that! But what about the rest of them? Could I actually get rid of them now? Most of them went, but to this day I still have several of her outfits in my basement. Pretty soon they too will go!

Sarah loved to have sleepovers. Many Friday nights we hosted sleepovers for between one and five girls. The girls loved the French toast Rich would fix them for breakfast. If the girls were not at our house, they would be at someone else's home on a Friday night. I can remember only one Friday night sleepover, during junior high, when I had to call parents to come and get their daughters at midnight. One of the girls, the ring-leader, tried to crawl out a basement window. I don't think the other girls would have followed, but it was important for them to know this was not acceptable behavior, and all the other parents agreed.

During Sarah's young years, most mothers did not work outside of home. The elementary school was just down the block from our home, and many moms were involved at school in various ways. This connection with Sarah's friends and their mothers formed very special bonds that lasted throughout grade school, junior high, and high school. A number of those special friendships still endure after all these years.

Sarah was baptized at Bethlehem Lutheran Church. Over the years she went to Sunday School and Hi-League there, and she was a member until she moved away. When she was in junior high, she started bringing several friends home for lunch after church on Sundays. This was a good time for Rich and me to go out to eat alone, as the girls loved making chicken noodle soup out of a package for their Sunday noon meal. These friends are in her life still.

There came a time when some of our friends from church decided to go camping together with their families; many had children Sarah's age. We did not own a tent or camper. I had never camped and Rich did not *want* to camp. But I felt that this would be another chance to bond as families. I believe Rich listened to God's prodding, and he agreed to buy a tent. So camping we did—in sunshine and in rain—until one trip when it rained all weekend long. I came home insisting that the next time I wanted to be two feet off the ground! I took another bookkeeping job, and we bought a camping trailer. The next time we went we were two feet off the ground, and we loved it! Rich grew to enjoy camping, and our camping companions have become lifelong friends. Looking back at our camping experiences, the church friends Sarah made— not only the kids her age, but their parents as well—have been her support, her prayer warriors, and her mentors all through her many years of struggling. At various times, I sent each family a short note thanking them for their support and asking them for some special prayer in whatever Sarah was going through at the time. *Thank you, God, for opening Rich's heart to buy that first tent!*

As a family, we were blessed with wonderful, supportive family and friends. Sarah did not know what a treasure she had in family and friends until she was much older, and they remain such a special part of her life.

While Sarah had many friends, I also have special memories of just the two of us spending time together. Pre-school days in the early hours each morning, after Dad went to work, were special. Those were the days of television's *Mr. Rogers, Captain Kangaroo*, and *Sesame Street*. With Sarah still in her pajamas, she would sit in my lap in Grandpa's rocking chair, and we would watch the TV programs together. Sarah loved puzzles, sticker books, and coloring; we spent many hours doing these together.

When she was four years old, I began taking her to the Fairview Hospital pool for swimming lessons. I did not know how to swim, and I was determined that Sarah would learn to swim and be comfortable in the water. She loved the water and did learn to swim. After her lessons, we would stop at the Minneapolis Art Institute and spend time just walking the halls. I'm pretty sure we spent more time observing the art exhibits than we did in the gift shop, even though she always talked me into visiting there as well. And, of course, in her later years, I was always guaranteed time together if I suggested shopping!

Sarah also spent time in pre-school while I took a small part-time job doing bookkeeping in our home. This evolved into a small home business, enabling me to be at home all the years Sarah was in school. Working at home also enabled me to be available for the activities she was interested in—and her interests were *many*. Her summers and after-school hours were spent in gymnastics, softball, track, ballet, tennis, skating, swimming, horseback riding, skiing, piano, church motion choir, Wendy Ward "modeling," Brownies, Girl Scouts, and many other church activities. She was a happy, busy girl!

Chapter 3

"MRS. HOLTE, YOU JUST CANNOT ACCEPT AN 'AVERAGE' CHILD!"

"God is ready to assume full responsibility for the life wholly yielded to Him." Andrew Murray

*W*e only prayed that Sarah's life at school could be as fulfilling as her social life. She was called a precocious child when she was in pre-school. In first grade she was so excited to be a "giraffe"—a member of the top reading group. But midway through the year she had dropped to the middle group, and by the end of first grade she had been moved to the "bears," the bottom reading group. I was puzzled and saddened, but not really alarmed at that point. We had read to her every night before bed while she was young. Friday nights usually meant a visit to the library, and we would arrive home loaded with books to read. Her sisters read to her when they were home and gave her books for her birthday and Christmas. She loved "browsing" through her books. We worked with her on reading skills each evening at home. I was sure reading would "click" for her very soon.

But to my dismay it did not.

Her reading did not improve, nor did her writing and comprehension. Spelling was also a very troublesome area for Sarah. After working with her on spelling the night before an assignment, I was so sure she would be successful the next day. However, by the next day, it was like the spelling words were totally erased from her memory. Completing written assignments was even more troubling—to me, but not to Sarah! At this point Sarah seemed not to be bothered at all with her poor school performance, but I certainly was. Throughout most of grade school and junior high, I was disheartened when I read the graded papers she brought home from school. Truly, I could not make sense of them! I would often cry when I read her workbooks and papers; she couldn't put two sentences together in any readable form. All of her written assignments came back with red ink all over them: "This was in no condition to hand in, it should have been proof-read and re-copied...Poorly organized... You make this mistake time after time...If you had proof-read carefully, you would have picked up sections that do not make sense." There were always big red Ds and Fs on her papers. But Sarah loved gym. And she loved her friends, who were always right there with her!

By then Sarah was in fourth grade. We never saw any of her work on the board or around the room when we visited school. Nor would we ever be elated to hear of her good work from any of her teachers. She was never chosen for any special responsibilities or assignments. We were never able to use the bumper sticker on our car: "Proud Parent of a Minneapolis School Honor Student!" At every teacher conference I was told Sarah just needed to work harder.

Now I *was* worried, and we began to suspect that she may have a learning problem. From fourth grade on, I became a constant visitor to the school. I spent many sessions with her teachers, special education consultant, and principal, pleading with them to give her some additional help. I would ask the special education consultant and principal for conferences. They became very annoyed with me and would only tell me, "No, she is not a great student, but she surely does not need any special help."

For me, one of the most crushing school meetings was a conference with Sarah's fifth grade teacher. Sarah and all of her friends couldn't wait to be in sixth grade because that is when they could be a school patrol. This was a *big deal*—an honor and a responsibility they really looked forward to. And, of course, everyone in sixth grade who wanted to be a patrol would be outfitted for the "job." Well, at this fifth-grade conference, I was told by the teacher that Sarah could not be a school patrol next year because her grades were not "good enough." I was so stunned and so absolutely confused that I began to cry. It made no sense to me. Sarah was a very responsible student, a pleasant girl, and one who would surely take this responsibility seriously. What did her grades have to do with responsibility? I think my reaction took the teacher by such surprise that she told me she would think about it and get back to me. Sarah *was* a school patrol in sixth grade at her elementary school. At the time, I decided not to tell Sarah about this encounter. Many years later, when she was about twenty-five years old, I told her that the only reason she was able to be a school patrol was because her mother cried!

When Sarah was in fifth grade, I called for one last meeting with the classroom teacher, the special education teacher, and the principal. I can still remember sitting around the oblong conference table looking at each one, praying that this time they would really *listen* and empathize with me. I told them we were going to take Sarah to Washburn Child Guidance Center for some special tutoring. I can still see the special education consultant looking directly at me and telling me, "Mrs. Holte, you just cannot accept an 'average' child!" They tried to convince us that we would be wasting our money if we decided to do that. Everyone else around the table agreed. But, we did it anyway.

Sarah spent a summer at Washburn Child Guidance Center. While she never objected to going, I never really knew if she felt good about it or was just going because we wanted her to. I remember that first summer when it came time for our vacation. We were going to interrupt her tutoring sessions for two weeks, and I was pretty sure she would be excited to be able to miss her studies for that time. However, to my surprise, she said she felt bad missing her tutoring, but would, of course, go on vacation with us. I was thrilled to hear she would miss it and immediately realized that she felt good to feel successful at something.

When Sarah was a young adult, I remember asking her how she had felt in those grade-school years, when she was doing so poorly and she knew all of her friends were high achievers and were getting all the accolades for their work in school. Her answer was quick and to the point: "I never even thought about it. I had all my friends, and that is all that mattered then." And all of Sarah's friends never left her and were certainly her strong supporters. However, as the years wore on and she continued to struggle in school, it did begin to matter to her. When she entered junior high, I began to feel the stress building. I remember her telling me later that others often would call her "stupid" and made fun of her for not being able to learn and for getting such poor grades.

Sarah began seventh grade at Anthony Junior High with all of her friends in the neighborhood. That summer she was on the Park Board softball team, where she made some new friends who were going to a different school, Southwest Junior High. When Sarah was at Anthony she kept in touch with these new friends, but her long-time friends from kindergarten were still her closest buddies.

However, now it was beginning to be very evident she was struggling, and school was beginning to overwhelm her. It was during seventh grade that she began to suffer from stomach problems, which, after testing, the doctors advised us were stress related. During this same time frame, she would oftentimes want to stay home from school because she "didn't feel well." Many a morning I would find her buried under the covers trying to convince me she was not well, and I would have to almost drag her out of bed.

I look back now and realize those years were the beginning of the Journey—the journey of a mother and her daughter with God!

Chapter 4

"I'M SO SORRY...CAN WE START OVER?"

"Every trial becomes a means of grace!" Author Unknown

This Journey was a journey with God, a strong-willed German-heritage mother, and a daughter with a mind of her own. Sarah fit Dr. James Dobson's description of the "strong-willed child" perfectly. Our older girls had left home to attend college or travel and so were not around during much of Sarah's growing-up years. I quickly learned that Sarah had an abundance of my forceful personality and not the gentle, tender, non-combative personality of her sisters. For years I had attended every parenting class available and had accumulated a shelf full of books on raising children. I wanted Sarah to be gentle, tender, loving, forgiving, and compassionate. Yet, at this age, Sarah was strong-willed, had a mind of her own, could be obnoxious and negative, resisted authority, loved to argue, was easily angered, wanted her own way, and didn't even seem to acknowledge us as her parents in public. But...she had tons of friends!

More than anything, though, I wanted Sarah to be a secure child of God and to have a personal relationship with Jesus. I wanted her life to be grounded and secure in Him, because I knew what was ahead for her in the big world out there. Then I read a new book on raising children. This book reminded me that thirteen-year-olds *are* loud, obnoxious, selfish, and seem to be uncaring. Thirteen–year-olds *do* act in public as if they don't even know their parents. They *do* act as if they don't want to be touched. In reality, they desperately crave their parents' love and need to be touched and hugged often. They long to be told over and over again that we love them! Before I read this book, I thought that we verbalized our love for Sarah well enough. I believed that she had received the message of our love. But now I began to be more deliberate about making *sure* she got the message. Every morning as she left for school, I would tell her I loved her—even if she slammed the door on her way out! When she came home from school, I would tell her that I loved her. Other days, as I dropped her off in the morning or picked her up after school, I would say, "Love you!" At bedtime I told her, "I love you," and again as I woke her each morning. Every note I left for her was signed "Love you!" You might think that was a little too much, that it would become meaningless and she would tire of hearing it, but to this day she signs all *her* notes that same way and often tells us she loves us.

I began to do little things just to let her know that she was loved. In fact, I felt the desire to do these little things even *more* after we had a disagreement or after a confrontation; I just needed to let her know that things were still okay. Some mornings after she left for school, I would make my way into her bedroom, make her bed (if I could get through the mess), and leave a note saying "I love you," just to let her know that our disagreement that morning didn't make any difference in my love for her. From time to time I would clean her room or hang up her clothes or pick up the bathroom, not so much when things were *good*, but when times were *bad* between us, or when she was having a lousy day.

Now, if you knew about my own strong-willed temperament, you would know that this did not come naturally to me. Sometimes I would be so mad at her after she left, I would say to myself, *Forget it. I don't really care!* Many times, as she slammed her bedroom door or the outside door when leaving, I would fume, *Let her do her own thing. I don't really care!* But God was changing me. So often—after having this "forget it, kid" feeling—an overwhelming emotion would overcome me. It was a feeling I can hardly explain, except to say that I felt such an intense love for Sarah that was not superficial, but came from deep down inside me. This is the feeling that would lead me to her messy bedroom...the feeling that would lead me to turn on her electric blanket on a cold night before she came in...the feeling that I wanted to do something for her just because I loved her, not because she deserved it. THIS WAS NOT HUMAN LOVE—IT HAD TO BE GOD'S LOVE!

Then, after an especially trying morning, as Sarah slammed the door on her way out, I found that I couldn't wait for her to come home! As she came in the door from school, I put my arms around her, hugged her, and said, "Sarah, I'm so sorry for this morning. Can we start all over?" I immediately felt her body loosen up, a half-smile *almost* crossed her face, and she said, "Okay." From that day on and throughout the rest of her days at home, we have relied on this special touch of God. Many days I waited for Sarah to come home from school after the door had "shut" especially hard on her way out that morning, or following a serious disagreement. I couldn't wait to put my arms around her and say, "Sarah, I'm so sorry about this morning," or "I'm so sorry about the way I acted," or "I'm so sorry about the way things turned out; please forgive me, and can we start over?" And then it was in her junior and senior years of high school that she often would get to me first and say, "Mom, I need a hug. I'm really sorry; can we start over?" She and I both knew that, from that moment on, everything in the past was wiped away. All the feelings and emotions that went along with our conflict were also gone, totally removed, and we were ready to pick up anew. Only God could have made that possible for both of us!

God began to reveal to me little ways to share my faith with Sarah. I wanted to encourage her, to share with her during the many times she struggled with her learning disabilities, but I needed guidance. I did not want to turn her off and hear her say, "Oh Mom!" I bought a figurine of a child in the palm of God's hand and put it in her bedroom. When she was struggling, I would often tell her that she was very small in God's big hand, and all He had to do was close His hand around her and she was secure and protected.

I also have little cards with the same picture and message. The picture is of a child in God's hand and the message is from Isaiah 49:15–16, which says, "*See! I will not forget you...I have carved you on the palm of My hand.*" When Sarah would leave for a weekend or a trip, I would always stick one of these cards in her suitcase with a note telling her how grateful I was that she belonged to God and that He was taking care of her when she was away from us. Years later, when she was away at school, she called home one night and said, "Mom, you know those cards with that verse from Isaiah? Would you send me some of them? My friend is going to have surgery and is so frightened; I want to give him one."

Another way God prompted me to encourage Sarah was through what I call my "mirror ministry." I began posting notes, sometimes on Sarah's bedroom mirror, but most often on the bathroom mirror—a verse or note of encouragement that I felt she needed to hear that day. I began doing this when Sarah was in junior high, and I continued to add or change the notes until the day she left our home. I was pretty sure she would ask me to take them down when her friends slept over, but to my surprise and delight, she never, ever asked to have them removed. Every now and then I would even hear her sharing the messages of these mirror notes with her friends.

It has been thirty years or more, but to this day, there are still notes on our bathroom mirror, although the verses have changed from time to time. To be honest, they are kind of tacky by now, but I cannot remove them because they still encourage me daily as well.

God gave me a new insight through another book I was reading. The author convinced me that Sarah was as good or as bad as *I* was good or bad. While dealing with my own emotions, I would often lose sight of the heavy burden she was carrying—her learning disabilities. I had to be reminded that together our little family of three was experiencing the tension of struggling with her disabilities. I was fully aware that it was much easier for her to keep a wonderful, smiling personality in front of her friends when she could release all her negative emotions at home. But I would too often lose sight of that and allow my emotions to take over anyway.

When Sarah was in the sixth grade, I remember watching her come up the walk to the back door, bracing myself for what was to come. I expected her to be moody, argumentative, and obstinate, so I was prepared for the battle! Then God got my attention through that book. Now that I understood what I was doing, I began to imagine her coming in smiling, fun, and loving. I began to meet her at the door, give her a hug, and tell her that I loved her. I can't even begin to express how it affected Sarah—and me!

Thank you…thank you…thank you, God!

Chapter 5

"MOM, I WANT TO CHANGE SCHOOLS!"

"Seek ye first the kingdom of God and His righteousness, and all else will be added unto you!" Matthew 6:33

*S*arah came down with mononucleosis in February of seventh grade and missed about three weeks of school. As she had been struggling in school already, this really set her back and made school even more miserable for her. But her friends continued to support her. In March of that year, soon after bringing home about thirty pink Valentine notes of admiration from friends, which was a fun custom at her junior high, just out of the blue she began talking about transferring to a new school. She had decided she would like to change from the neighborhood junior high to the school where some of her Park Board friends attended. We didn't pay any attention to the talk until we realized she was serious.

We were stunned to think she would really leave all her good friends to begin at a school where she knew very few kids. She was soon absolutely obsessed with the idea and, just like us, her friends were bewildered. Rich and I puzzled and struggled over the meaning of all of this. For no apparent reason, she was willing to leave all that was important to her for the unknown.

I wrestled and wrestled with Sarah's desire to change schools. It became a powerful growth process for me, an exercise in letting go and trusting God, the God into whose hands I had placed her those many years ago.

When Sarah was about ten years old, I had begun to seriously search for Christian books on bringing up children. I also spent more time on my knees, and my time alone in the morning was spent in Bible study and devotions. A local Christian radio station became a regular resource for spiritual teaching. I specifically remember listening to a presentation on the topic of Raising Daughters, which made an impact at that very important time in raising my daughter. I knew I needed God's guidance and direction, especially at this time in her life.

Something others may have found odd or weird became very special to me during these years. Each day, before I even began my devotions, after everyone had left for the day, I would climb back upstairs to take my bath. I'm not at all sure how this special bathtub time began. But I remember clearly having a similar bathtub ritual when, as a young adult, I taught a high school Sunday School class. On Saturday nights, I would spend a long time in the bathtub preparing and reviewing my lessons for the next morning. I have special memories of the insights I received for my lessons during this time in the bathtub. Since that time, I would often retreat to the bathtub when I needed to talk with God and search for answers. It was there that I gained insight and peace about the direction we were to take when making a decision. God never speaks to me audibly, nor does He write on the wall or send a note floating down, but I do know He speaks to me in ways that I cannot explain.

Now I needed to talk with God and search for his direction. *Sarah wants to change schools, God. What should we do?* And so, to the bathtub I went! And what a peace came over me when the thought (from God) came to me that I should go to her school, seek the advice of the school counselor, and *follow it!*

That very afternoon, I was at the school meeting with Sarah's counselor; I knew that following her direction would be the answer. I was pretty certain, however, that the counselor would question the idea of pulling Sarah out of this school next year for no real reason. We would also have to get permission from the other school to enroll her there. Despite any obstacles, I knew I was willing to take whatever advice she gave us. To my utter surprise, after listening to the whole story, the counselor said, "If she is willing to give up the known for the unknown and begin a new school, you really should let her go." I left school that afternoon with such peace, knowing that the right decision had been provided. When we told Sarah of our decision to let her go, she was delighted and began making plans for the next year.

Amazed at this process, I told my friend that it was puzzling and almost bizarre, but I knew God was in charge and that He was taking hold of Sarah's life. I felt strongly that Sarah's life was going to change, yet nothing seemed to make sense; it all seemed so strange. While this is getting ahead of our story, looking back, we now know what a powerful thing God did at that very moment in time, because this decision truly *was* the beginning of Sarah's personal journey with God. If we had not followed God's guidance at this point, all the following events would never have happened.

Sarah's friends were puzzled and bewildered with her decision as well. They tried to convince her to stay with them, but Sarah transferred the next year in eighth grade. Her year started out well, and she made many new friends. However, after the first few months, her life began to go downhill. School was more difficult for her, and her grades got worse. I again asked for a school conference. It was at this conference that I became alarmed with the English teacher's comment that Sarah was daydreaming in class, just could not focus and that he believed she needed help. He informed me that she had failed the English Assessment test for all eighth graders. And after that she was placed in an "English as a Second Language" class. This transition was very disturbing to her.

Sarah had made many new friends in the beginning of the school year, but as the year progressed, she no longer seemed to fit in with the new crowd. She would come home from school all alone, she never seemed to smile, and the phone never rang. And she failed a couple of classes that year.

Most mornings I would sit at the piano after Sarah left for school, playing and singing some of my favorite songs — singing and sobbing. One of my favorite songs, written by Civilla D. Martin in 1904, that I would sing over and over was "God Will Take Care of You":

> Be not dismayed whate'er betide
> God will take care of you
> Beneath His wings of love abide
> God will take care of you
>
> *Refrain:*
> God will take care of you
> Through every day, o'er all the way
> He will take care of you
> God will take care of you
>
> Through days of toil when heart doth fail
> God will take care of you
> When dangers fierce your path assail
> God will take care of you.
>
> All you may need He will provide
> God will take care of you
> Nothing you ask will be denied
> God will take care of you
>
> No matter what may be the test
> God will take care of you
> Lean, weary one, upon His breast
> God will take care of you

Each morning I would kneel at Sarah's bed, turning her over to God again and again—knowing, but often questioning, that He was in control. As hard as it was, deep inside I still knew that we had done the right thing. It was at this time in my life that a friend introduced me to the "Praise" tapes: praise songs from the Maranatha! Singers, Ray Boltz, and others. Day after day I would listen to the messages of those praise songs. God kept me very close to Him. As I sang and listened to the messages on the tapes, the words finally soaked in and gave me real peace—a peace which "passes all understanding." Some of the many messages that were especially powerful during those days were:

"Seek Ye First the Kingdom of God"
"In His Time"
"The Shepherd Song"
"Another Child to Hold"
"Always Be a Child"

God was telling me that if I would quit dwelling on myself (and my loved ones, Sarah in particular) and instead *praise* and *worship* Him, put Him *first* in my life, then He would take care of the rest. Specifically, He was telling me, "Think on Me, and in My time all will be well." I had to release Sarah in faith and believe that God was in control. He was teaching me to praise and thank Him, not for the way things were right now necessarily, but for Him alone and what He meant to me. The Father wanted me to praise and thank Him for Sarah, and for what He would be doing for her in the future. In "The Shepherd Song," when I pictured Him carrying Sarah in His arms, how could I possibly worry? Many songs convinced me that Sarah would always be His child, and during many moments of anxiety, I was comforted that He was always holding her in His hands.

He taught me to actually sing out loud—I used Sarah's Walkman, hung around my neck, and earplugs. No matter what I was doing, I could use the Walkman, and most of each day during Sarah's years of struggling, I was singing and praising God with the "Praise" tapes. Sarah would come home and catch me singing at the top of my voice with earplugs in my ears, and she would laugh at me—because I really can't sing! I'm convinced that even though she didn't actually hear the words, she still caught the spirit of the messages God was revealing to me through those tapes.

Chapter 6

"I'M NOT GOING TO THAT SCHOOL WHERE ALL THE KIDS HAVE MONEY, WEAR FANCY CLOTHES, AND SIT AROUND AND TALK ABOUT GOD!"

"In his heart a man plans his course, but the Lord deter-mines his steps." Proverbs 16:9

Eighth grade at Southwest did not get any easier for Sarah as the year went on. But God continually reminded me in my daily time with Him that she was in His hands and things would happen in His timing, according to His plan for her life.

Rich and his family grew up in South Minneapolis, and he had graduated from Minnehaha Academy, a small private Christian high school in his neighborhood. This school was very familiar to everyone, and Sarah knew a few friends and family who were going there. The thought had entered our minds when Sarah was struggling through seventh grade that maybe a school like Minnehaha Academy, with smaller classes and a compassionate staff, would be good for Sarah. We hoped that they might be able to provide some academic help. We actually had presented the idea to her, but she would have no part of it, so we dismissed it. Besides, it was so expensive!

But now, in about January of her eighth-grade year, and again for no apparent reason, she suggested she might like to go to Minnehaha. We, of course, were thrilled. As you may have already guessed, though, as more time passed at Southwest and she made a few more good friends, she changed her mind again. She really didn't want to go there next year. However, at this point Rich and I had made up our minds that the change to a smaller Christian school for her learning problems was what we wanted for her. When we presented to her that we had made this decision, she absolutely refused to listen—there was no way she would go to that school, even though she was the one who had originally suggested it! I'm not sure how, but we did convince her to at least visit the school during the February Open House for prospective students. Sarah spent that school day visiting classes with other students. She came home all the more adamant about not going to that school, where "all the kids have money, wear fancy clothes, and sit around and talk about God! No way!"

After spending much time and prayer on this idea, we still truly felt Minnehaha Academy would be a better place for Sarah with her learning problems. But we would still have to figure out how to pay for it, and how we were going to get her there. Again, we desperately needed an answer. Earlier I had told God that we could not afford it, but if He really wanted her to go there, I prayed that He would make it known to us. I believed that if He did want Sarah at that school, then He would probably send a new job my way. However, I was also reminded of a decision I had just made. As a self-employed bookkeeper, I often got clients through referrals from a local accounting firm. But in the last few months, I had told the accounting firm that I had all the clients I needed right now and not to refer any more to me.

It was now spring and we were wrestling with this more intently because a decision had to be made very soon about enrolling Sarah in Minnehaha Academy. One morning I was sitting at the kitchen table having my devotions and facing the plaque on the wall, which read, "He gives His best to those who leave the choice to Him." *Lord*, I prayed, *help me with this decision, but let it be Your choice!* I shared with God how confused we were about this decision and that apparently He didn't want her to change schools because He had not provided another job. (But after all, isn't that what I had just told the accounting firm I did not want?) I prayed, *God, if you really want Sarah to go to Minnehaha, you will have to bring me another job.* As I continued my devotions, the telephone rang. It was Greg from the accounting firm. "Donna, would you be interested in another job?" Although I could barely talk as tears were running down my face, I immediately shared the news. "Greg, do you know that you have just been an answer to prayer?" Greg is a Christian, and after telling him the background, he was astounded as well and was able to rejoice with me in this very special work of God. Of course I told him, "Yes, I would be very grateful for a new job." After hanging up the phone, I pretty much fell apart and fell on my knees, crying and thanking God for this very, very personal and powerful touch in our lives!

I shared this story with Rich when he came home from work. We knew now, of course, that this was our answer. But Sarah had been fighting us all the way. There was *no way* she would ever consider going to that school! Did we have the nerve to follow what we knew to be God's guiding and possibly risk our relationship with our daughter? *God, help!* And He did. He again met me in the bathtub; again, such peace came over me with the thought that He brought to me: *Talk with the Minnehaha admissions director, tell him she really does not want to be there, and ask if they would still want her to come.* I immediately got out of the tub, picked up the phone, made an appointment, and visited with Mr. Norby that very afternoon. He told me that if we felt we wanted her there, then we should send her, and they would handle it from there. I can't tell you the peace I again felt when I walked out of that school.

Wow, God, now I really need your help! I knew exactly what I needed to do, but oh how nervous I was! I met Sarah at the bus stop that afternoon. We went into the house, sat down at the table, and I told her I needed to talk with her. "Sarah, Dad and I have decided that you will be going to Minnehaha Academy next year." It took just seconds and all hell broke loose! She yanked the tablecloth off the table, and everything on it went flying as she yelled, "I am NOT going to Minnehaha! No way! You can't make me! I am NOT going!" She was absolutely wild and furious. In an unbelievable rage, she ran from the table to the sofa in the family room yelling, "I am NOT going! I am <u>NOT</u> going!" I truly believe that Satan had her in his clutches for just those few minutes. God allowed him to do that, and then He took control again. It was then that the miracle happened.

Sarah went to the sofa and sat down. I went to sit beside her, planning to calm her down. She sat there for a few seconds and then I heard: "You will have to let me dress like them." And then, "Can I still get my new skates?" I was overwhelmed and could hardly believe what I had just heard. Had she really said this? In my heart, I knew this was all God's plan!

I assured her that we would let her buy a new sweater and turtleneck (like they were wearing at Minnehaha). Yes, she could continue her skating lessons. We discussed that I would drive her to school every day, as a bus was not available in our area. And, probably most importantly, I told her that she would only have to try it for the first semester. After that time, if she did not like it she would not have to continue. We went out shopping that very day, and there was never a question from then on about going to Minnehaha. And after this powerful touch from God, she continued to be calm and, when her Dad got home from work, we shared that she, in fact, was going to go to Minnehaha Academy beginning the next fall.

I truly believe that God allowed Satan to take hold of Sarah for those few minutes and then He said, "That's enough!" And from that moment on, God has continued to be in control of her life. She has been obedient to Him ever since, even though she really is not always aware of it.

Thank you...thank you...thank you, God!

And this I believe, from a Frances Roberts quote: "Just as surely as ye make Me happy with your praising...ye shall make the enemy most unhappy! Satan has no power whatsoever over a praising Christian!"[4] Satan truly did not want Sarah to go to that school "where they sit around and talk about God."

Chapter 7

"YOU'RE NOT GOING TO TAKE
ME OUT OF MINNEHAHA,
ARE YOU?"

"God's plans are unshakable!" Psalms 33:10

*I*n my mind, Sarah's first weeks at Minnehaha in ninth grade were questionable. She was not complaining, but she didn't come home each day excited either. While she was making new friends, we were never quite sure what was going on in her head. We suspected that, from the beginning, she had planned to stay only the first semester. I continued to pray for her, then a special "God-touch" happened later in the fall. She asked if she could buy an Amy Grant tape. I didn't know who Amy Grant was or that she sang Christian music with a wonderful message. This was a real change from the music Sarah had been listening to with her friends from Southwest. Of course I bought a tape for her, said a prayer of thanksgiving, and asked that this message would speak to her—and it did! Later she *did* sit around with her friends and "talk about God."

The fall semester was coming to an end, and I was still not certain what Sarah was thinking. We, of course, would honor our decision to allow her to go back to Southwest after the first semester if she chose to. I picked her up from school one day in the middle of December. She got in the car beside me and, after riding in silence for a short while, looked at me and asked, "You're not going to take me out of Minnehaha, are you?"

Thank you…thank you…thank you, God!

However, academically, Sarah did have a horrible ninth-grade year. She was nearly failing all of her courses. I visited the school several times to talk with a counselor. While they were pleased to see she had many friends and that her social life was not lacking, they too were very concerned about her academic performance. Sarah truly loved Minnehaha and her new friends. Again, she was involved in weekend parties and sleepovers. Her teachers offered as much help as they could, but she still struggled each day in class and with assignments.

Sarah's counselor, Sue, called me to the school one day in November. She was ready to refer us to a private tutor. I was so encouraged to be moving in the right direction for Sarah. While I was afraid that Sarah would be unwilling to take this step, I knew that she really liked and respected Sue and would be open to her advice. I also believe that Sarah was so mentally and emotionally exhausted from struggling that she might be truly eager to check this out. Sue referred us to Educational Specialists, a counseling and tutoring service, and I made an appointment the very next week. To this day, I cannot say the names Cookie and Elayne without a real tug at my heart.

We met with Cookie, who was the director. She was anxious to do extensive testing for Sarah. We came back several days later after school, and I waited in the office as Sarah spent about two hours in testing with Cookie. Later in the week, Rich and I both sat in Cookie's office while she explained all Sarah's testing to us. I don't think Rich really accepted everything Cookie was telling us, but for me it was a relief—finally there was an answer! After very extensive testing, Sarah was diagnosed with a severe learning disability: dyslexia. We later learned she also had attention deficit disorder, commonly known as ADD. We were introduced to Elayne, who would be her tutor. They were both astounded that Sarah had been able to keep up with her grade at all, especially at Minnehaha Academy. She was in the ninth grade and was reading at a second-grade level! We left there pretty drained, but for me it was the answer to many long years of anxiety. Now that we had identified the causes of Sarah's struggles, we could begin to provide her with the long overdue help she needed.

Sarah was not with us at that appointment, but after she began her tutoring, she was helped to understand everything about her disabilities. She saw her tutor, Elayne, for three one-hour sessions a week. During the summer months, she went nearly every day. I brought a book and read during each of Sarah's sessions, so I got a fair amount of reading done during those three and a half years of tutoring—the remainder of her high school years. Elayne was troubled that Sarah had not been diagnosed earlier and had not been able to take advantage of tutoring when she was in elementary and junior high school. Because tutoring help started this late in Sarah's life, Elayne was limited to helping Sarah maintain her day-to-day assignments, without providing her with skills to improve her learning. At this point, that is all we could ask. Sarah loved Elayne, who made her feel very special. Because of this, she never, ever objected to going for tutoring.

Identifying Sarah's struggles helped me in my next venture. I spent many hours searching for information and learning as much as I could about dyslexia and attention deficit disorder (ADD). They truly could be devastating disabilities if one just accepted them without trying to understand them. Elayne was so good in helping Sarah understand her strengths as well as her weaknesses—and she does have many, many strengths!

Sarah had many ups and downs during her high school years, but Elayne was always there for her. Sarah has a bond with Elayne to this day, and Elayne has remained Sarah's mentor and friend. She was, however, uncertain if Sarah would be able to handle college; but Sarah was determined to try! Inspired by Sarah, Elayne put aside her doubts, encouraging her and preparing her in every way she could toward this goal. I then began another search, for an advisor to help us decide on a college that would be suitable for Sarah. During her junior year in high school, Sarah spent time with Joanne, an educational specialist who helped her talk through her goals and made suggestions on colleges. College was certainly on Sarah's horizon!

Chapter 8

"CALIFORNIA, HERE WE COME!"

"I will instruct you, says the Lord, and guide you along the best pathway for your life." Psalms 32:8

*I*n June of 1985, the summer before Sarah graduated from high school, she and I began a two-week trek to California to visit several colleges that we were interested in. The night before we were to leave, I went and rented a car. Because of work, Rich was not able to go with us. The plan was for Sarah and me to share the driving and make several stops to visit family and friends along the way. But I got a surprise while signing the rental papers when I learned that anyone under twenty-one years old could not drive the rental car. Oh, well, I was sure it would not be a problem. I could drive the entire way if Sarah would keep me company. I *did* drive the entire way to California…while Sarah *slept* most of the way! We had an uneventful trip, and we still remember fondly this special time together.

Why were we headed for California? For only one reason: Sarah wanted to go to school "in the sun." She did not like

Minnesota winters and saw her college choice as a chance to be in the warm weather. I can imagine that in her mind was only one thought: *I may just stay out there—in the sun!* Sarah did not know anyone at any of the colleges we were to visit; she didn't even know anyone in California. We planned to visit four colleges and had made appointments with each of the admissions counselors. At the end of one week, we had been to three of the schools and had pretty much eliminated two of them, but the third was a real possibility. She was impressed with California Lutheran in Thousand Oaks, but probably more because she really wanted to locate near Los Angeles. We had one more college to visit: Westmont College, a Christian college up the coast in Santa Barbara.

During the whole process of thinking about colleges and locations, I felt such mixed emotions. Throughout all of Sarah's life, I had hung on to the promises that she was in God's hands and He would guide and direct her. After all, isn't that exactly what I had prayed for when she was an infant? And all her life I only wanted her to be happy. Now she was choosing to move very far from home. How did I feel about that? As a mom, I was sad, a little nervous, unsettled; yet if she was going to be happy here, this is exactly what I had been praying for. I admired Sarah; if she chose a college far from home, knowing no one there, what a brave and confident child she was. God truly had to be guiding her!

Santa Barbara, here we come! It was a beautiful day in June with a clear sky and bright sunshine. We arrived in

Santa Barbara and realized the college was a drive into the mountains. Sarah will tell you today that it was the beautiful drive up Hot Springs Road in the mountains with our back to the ocean that convinced her about Westmont College, even before we arrived on campus. Westmont is located right in the mountains and you can see the Pacific Ocean when you look out the second-floor dorm window. What more could she want? We had an appointment with the admissions director and admissions counselor. We had her high school transcript with us, which they studied very carefully. Sarah's grade point average was very low—she later went on to graduate from high school with a grade point average of only 1.9 on a 4.0 scale—but they were also aware of her learning disabilities.

We later learned that Westmont College has a very high academic rating and accepts only students with high grade point averages. In fact, the school had accepted only one other student with a learning disability, and at that time he was the student body president. But they had also made a decision that they would no longer accept learning-disabled students. The city of Montecito, where the college was actually located, had an enrollment quota for the college, an additional criterion compelling Westmont to be very selective in choosing their students.

Sarah and I spent time together with the admissions director and counselor, then Sarah had her time alone with them. She left that meeting smiling and comfortable, with the promise that they would be getting back to us by next spring. She absolutely fell in love with the school, the staff, the campus, and the setting, confirming that this was where she wanted to be for the next four years. We arrived back home and now we had to wait. What would their decision be? Sarah was very nervous!

Waiting for a decision was going to be hard! Westmont would make their decision in early spring. That spring, Sarah was invited to spend the week of spring break at a Florida condo with friends and their parents. Because she had no cell phone at that time, Sarah had to stay in touch with us when she was in Florida with a telephone calling card. She knew this was about the time Westmont would be calling to inform her of their decision—definitely another incentive to call home often. Each day while she was gone I got a little more anxious; surely they would be calling soon. Finally, the phone rang one evening at about 7 p.m. "Mrs. Holte, this is Tina from Westmont. We have decided to accept Sarah for the coming year." To say that I was elated would be an understatement!

Thank you...thank you...thank you, God!

I hung up the phone in tears and could hardly wait for Sarah to call. Why hadn't she called yet? It seemed forever before she finally called at about 10 p.m. "Sarah, you're in! You are going to Westmont next year!" Not being there in person with her, I can only imagine what she was feeling. She would be going to Westmont for her freshman year of college!

Only later did we learn why we had to wait so long for

Westmont's decision. The admissions director had to approach the board *three* times before he convinced them to accept Sarah into Westmont College! We are so grateful to him!

Sarah's senior year at Minnehaha was a struggle academically, but again, the friends she made there kept her going and contributed to who she is today. They continue to be her lifelong friends, no matter what part of the country she is living in. Sarah graduated from Minnehaha Academy in June of 1986. Even though she was fourth from the bottom of her class, we were extremely proud of her and were determined to help her follow her dream to go to college. We had a graduation open house, and we all celebrated!

Chapter 9

"I WILL EVEN MISS THE LOUD MUSIC, CLUTTERED BATHROOM, DISHES IN THE KITCHEN, AND SHOES IN THE HALLWAY!"

"Keep your eyes upon Jesus!" Author Unknown

*I*n August 1986, Sarah and I were again off to California in a rented car, this time with Rich along. We would arrive at Westmont a couple of weeks before school began because Tina had encouraged Sarah to take part in Inoculum, a two-week orientation program for freshmen. This experience was meant to be a time for freshmen to bond while hiking in the Sierra Madre Mountains. Although it was extremely challenging physically, Sarah loved it and made many friends before school even started. Even though she sustained a toe injury from her hiking boots, which laid her up later in the year, she would not have traded the experience.

Her dorm was situated right in the middle of the beautiful Santa Ynez Mountains. When looking out the window of her second-floor dorm room, we could see the ocean, which was only a ten-minute drive away. It truly was a beautiful campus. Sarah shared this view with many classmates who became her lifelong friends.

Leaving Sarah at Westmont was an emotional experience for me. While I knew she was going to be very happy there and that Westmont was where I wanted her to be, I also knew that returning home to an empty house was going to be very hard! I left Sarah the following letter on her bed as we were leaving her:

> *I will make my people strong with power from*
> *me! They will go wherever they wish, and wher-*
> *ever they go, they will be under my personal care.*
> *Zechariah 10:12*

> *Dear Sarah,*
>
> *I'm not looking forward to returning home to our empty house. We will miss so much your neat smile and cheery disposition, and just the fun and loving person you are deep inside.*
>
> *You know, I'm sure I will even miss the loud music, cluttered bathroom, dishes in the kitchen, and shoes in the hallway!*
>
> *But, how can we really be sad when you are so happy? We have prayed and prepared for eighteen years for the day when you can be independent, and we are so proud of you! You have followed the Lord and He has truly*

blessed you. We thank Him daily for that. He has "called you by name and you are in His hands."

You know you are in our prayers many times a day. We are so at peace because you are a "child of God" and He cares for you! We love you more than you can really know!

KEEP YOUR EYES UPON JESUS!
We love you so!

Coming back to Minneapolis without Sarah was so hard! My office is on the second floor of our home looking out to the front. Each day for the past two years, Sarah had driven herself to school and from my office window I would see her come home. Now I would look out and feel so lonely, knowing she would not be driving up. It was *so* quiet in our house! I heard myself telling someone, shortly after she had left, that I could not believe other people had gone through these very same emotions and I never knew it. How did they do it? And not only was Sarah away at college, but our other two daughters—Kathy and Debby—were now married and beginning their own families, so we did not see them as often as before either. So it was a lonely time for me.

There were no cell phones in 1986 (or at least we did not have one), and in those days long-distance calls from our home phone were very expensive. Plus, I was very conscious of how often I called Sarah at college, lest I be made to feel like an "overprotective" mother. When we did talk, I was continually thankful that she was still very happy.

College was certainly a challenge for Sarah. She relied from time to time on Elayne, her high school tutor, who she worked with via telephone when she had a written assignment. Her friends were also very eager to help her with reading assignments. When Sarah came home for Christmas during her freshman year, she could hardly wait to get back. When we picked her up at the airport, she met us with a big smile; her year was going great, at least with her friends. But college life wasn't perfect. When she returned to school for the second semester, she began to struggle academically.

All of the Westmont staff was very aware of Sarah's learning disabilities and was exceptional in trying to meet her needs. Each instructor had read her profile before accepting her in the class and had made accommodations for her as best they could. This was college, however, and she was expected to do college work. She knew this, of course, and was determined to continue.

And continue she did. She continued to struggle in school, and then one day she called home with another issue. The knee she had hurt in ballet was now beginning to bother her, and she found a strange lump on her upper back. We advised her to begin therapy on her knee. Knowing she needed to have the lump looked at, and not knowing a doctor in Santa Barbara, I called a local hospital and asked to talk with several nurses. I have always believed hospital nurses, who work day-in and day-out with the doctors, were probably the best source for referrals. I told them about Sarah, that she was from Minneapolis without a doctor in California, and asked them for a recommendation. Actually, several nurses recommended the same doctor, so Sarah scheduled a visit with him. It was nothing serious, but he did recommend it be removed then rather than wait until she came home for the summer. That sort of shook me for a bit, especially because I was not there with her. But again, I knew I had to leave her in God's hands. On the morning of the surgery, I talked with the doctor and prayed with Sarah over the telephone. This surgery was just another hurdle in Sarah's struggles—and another test of the faithfulness of God in her life! In the end, she did just fine; the lump turned out to be benign and was removed without further treatment.

That summer, Sarah came home and worked as a waitress at a local restaurant. She has always been outgoing, so this job was a perfect fit for her. And she discovered something new about herself—a new gift! She found that when she was taking orders, she did not have to write out the ticket; she could remember each person's order at the table. This was pretty amazing to me. She had several waitressing jobs after this and found that her amazing memory was a true gift.

For me, Sarah's discovery triggered a memory of my own. I realized that I had seen this gift of hers before, but had not recognized it at the time. One day, when Sarah was only in grade school, I was making a telephone call before we went shopping at a nearby mall. She was anxiously waiting for me by the telephone. There was no answer at the other end, so I repeated the telephone number to myself so I could try the call again when we reached the mall. But, of course, by the time we got into our car, drove the half-mile to the mall, got out of the car, and walked into the mall, I had forgotten the telephone number. But Sarah had not! She had heard me repeat the number out loud, and she still remembered it when we got there. And, of course, she got it right. I certainly did not recognize this as a gift back then. Now it was showing up again, and what a gift as a waitress.

After being home for the summer, Sarah was just as excited as ever to be going back to Westmont for her sophomore year. While getting back with her friends in the fall was great, she struggled with her assignments even more than she had in her freshman year. Her professors were wonderful and did as much as they could to help her, but I could tell she was beginning to get very discouraged. She called home one day and was very distraught. One of her instructors expressed to her that he just could not understand why she "could not read or write." This was a major blow to her, but she was determined not to give up.

Sarah worked hard at school until it was time to fly home for Christmas. It was always great to have her back home, even for a few weeks. We always have a great Christmas with all our family together. But I noticed that she was anxious to get back to school. I wondered to myself, *Could it be just to get out of the cold?* I didn't really think so; she truly loved getting back with her friends. Sarah finished her sophomore year and again came home to waitress at the same restaurant as the previous year. By the end of the summer she was ready to begin her junior year at Westmont College.

Chapter 10

"THE SPELLING WAS PERFECT, BUT I COULDN'T MAKE ANY SENSE OF YOUR PAPER!"

"Show me the path where I should go, O Lord; point out the right road for me to walk. Lead me...teach me."

Psalms 25:4

True to her nature, Sarah began her junior year upbeat and positive. Her Westmont friends had become such a special part of her life and were always so supportive. I'm not at all sure they ever really knew her struggles; they loved her and accepted her for just who she was! Those friends contributed to her success in life and to the special person she has become. They have remained in her life to this day.

As I look back through the year, I realize that it was during this semester that everything, outside of her social life, began to fall apart. One day I pushed the button on the answering machine and heard: "Moooommm! Mom, I'm stressed and I want to come home!" A number of years ago, I might have fallen apart and thought about bringing her home on the first plane. But I knew I had the choice to turn her over to God and say, *God, I'm so glad she belongs to You, and that You are in control of her life. You will have to take over now.* I had to leave her in God's hands and trust Him with this decision. My prayer was answered. The next day she was again ready to "take up the fight" and continue. Yes, she assured me, she really did want to stay in school.

However, as the semester wore on, things did not get any better. When Sarah was in high school, we had bought her a Walkman to listen to books on tape, hoping this would help in learning. However, this did not help in college because none of her textbooks were on tape. At Westmont, we bought her a computer with "Spell Check," hoping this would help with writing papers. It did help with spelling, of course, but she remembers to this day (and her professor remembers, as well) one of the final blows to her ego. After handing back a paper, the professor was quick to tell her how absolutely unreadable it really was. She asked him if the spelling was okay. "Yes," he said, "the spelling was perfect, but I couldn't make any sense of your paper." She was devastated!

Sarah's life went from bad to worse that year. During the second semester, she called home with more bad news: the knee she injured in ballet was hurting again, she had discovered another lump on her back, she had a mole that was doing "funny" things, and she was gaining unwanted weight from the medication she was taking to treat an ovarian cyst. On top of that, she wanted to know: what was the terrible pain in her leg? This again shook me some.

Not only did it shake me, but it also puzzled me. During all of Sarah's growing years, she had never been sick or had any physical complaints. The one exception was her bout of mononucleosis, but she had never had the stomach flu, a cold, a sore throat, an earache, or anything else to keep her from going to school. What was going on with her body now? I knew that once again I needed to turn Sarah's troubles over to God. We decided to wait until she came home for Christmas to have her visit our doctor here. The rest of the semester was really tough for her—classes were difficult, and she was physically, mentally, and emotionally exhausted. She couldn't study because she was in such pain from the ovarian cyst, and therefore she failed tests and got poor grades on her assignments. She began to call home again and again because she could hardly take it all. I would almost panic each time the telephone rang for fear it was Sarah with another traumatic issue. Sarah now calls this the semester of "The Meltdown!"

It was during these times that I would find myself on my knees many times during the day, crying out to God, *Thank you, God, that Sarah is Your child and that You are in control of her life!* A friend once asked me if I often asked God, *Why?* I could honestly say that, while I did not ask why, I surely did ask, *When?* I also relied on a song by the Maranatha Singers on my "Praise" tapes. This song, titled "In His Time," spoke to me so deeply, gave me strength, and spoke words that I have hung onto ever since. Through these simple lyrics—based off the verse in Ecclesiastes 3:11 that says "[God] has made everything beautiful in its time"—God was telling me that He does just what He says...in *His* time. He truly "makes all things beautiful in His time." I knew in my heart that God loved Sarah much more than I did, and He wanted the very best for her; but not only did He *want* the best for her, He also *knew* what was best for her. And He would provide the best for Sarah—in His time! Once again, I would leave her in His hands and TRUST!

I am convinced that, because He was holding her, she always seemed to bounce back and gain a peace that was unexplainable and enduring through the course of it all. Despite "The Meltdown," she planned to stay at Westmont.

However, as Rich and I began to think about everything that was going on in Sarah's life, we made our own decisions for her. Because of all her physical problems, as well as her academic struggles, we finally suggested she not go back after the first semester. I believe she was privately relieved to hear us say this, because she readily agreed it would be for the best. She began to think about applying to Augsburg College in Minneapolis for the second semester.

I talked with Westmont's president, Dr. Winter, and several others there and we all felt good about the decision to leave Westmont at that time. And surprisingly, Sarah seemed to be at peace with this decision. She felt sad to leave her faithful college friends, but she knew that she probably would not survive the pressure if she tried to finish at Westmont. The professors and staff had been so good to her, had supported her in so many ways, and also were sorry to see her leave. But they also knew this was probably the best decision for Sarah's future.

Chapter 11

"MOM, I WANT TO GO BACK!"

"For I know the plans I have for you, says the Lord.
They are plans for good and not for evil, to give you
a future and a hope."
Jeremiah 29:11

We met Sarah at the plane before Christmas, sad but knowing that she was, once again, embarking on a new chapter in her life. Sarah was okay with it and at peace as well. She spent the Christmas holiday planning her next steps, and immediately after Christmas she sent in her application to Augsburg College. She also enrolled in a weight-loss clinic, returned to her waitressing job, began saving for a car, and started "settling in," now that she was home to stay. She went to her gynecologist to check the ovarian cyst and was very relieved to hear the cyst had, in fact, disappeared. She also made an appointment to have the "funny" mole removed. As much as she missed her Westmont friends, she seemed at peace with beginning her new journey back in Minneapolis.

The first Monday in January was her gynecologist appointment. After returning home with the good news that the cyst had disappeared, she recalled that the following day, Tuesday, was the day her friends would be starting the second semester at Westmont—without her. I was not prepared for what happened next.

Late that night, at about 11 p.m., I was still working in my office when Sarah came in. She sat down on my lap at my desk and asked, "Mom, what am I doing? I am here and all my friends are back in California. I miss them so much. I really think I want to go back. Should I?" *WOW!* I thought, *now what?* We spent the next hour and a half talking...and talking...and talking about what was going on in her mind.

I had always wanted Sarah to be at Westmont, but only if she wanted to be there and felt that she could do it. Now she was telling me that she wanted to continue even if it would be hard. She had made so many neat friends who were so supportive of her, and the faculty and staff were there for her as well. She really wanted to give it another try. I believe that her renewed determination was the result of this time of rest that Sarah had been given. Just as important was her relief after hearing the cyst had disappeared and the mole was being taken care of. I believe she felt "renewed and refreshed" and was now able to move on again. She and I continued to struggle that night in my office, trying to decide what was best. I asked her if she could give up earning money for a car and the chance to lose weight at the clinic. Yes, she said she really would give up the car and the weight-loss clinic if she could go back to Westmont.

However, we realized that there were still a number of obstacles to her return. Sarah had learned to see God's activity in her life and to pray for God to guide her and for His will in her life. And now we knew we would have to turn this over to Him. And we did. If things did not work out to go back to Westmont, she would know that God wanted her to stay in Minneapolis, and she was willing to accept that. So we listed the things to be worked out:

1. We would have to share this with her Dad in the morning, and he would have to be in agreement with it. Would money be a problem now after not planning for her return to Westmont? Would he think this was absurd after all that had gone on?

2. Would she even be able to get back in to Westmont? We decided the first step would be to call the Admissions Office in the morning.

3. Would the manager at her job understand or resent that she would not fulfill her commitment?

4. Could she get her money back from the weight-loss clinic?

5. The mole would have to be removed in California.

6. Class was starting in the morning; could she book a plane ticket quickly to get there as soon as possible?

7. Finally, there would have to be a dorm room available for her, as she had already given hers up.

We went to bed around 1 a.m., and I'm sure neither of us really slept. I spent much of the night praying. The next day...

1. We talked with Dad before he left for work in the morning, and to our relief and surprise, he was on board and thought this was a good idea.

2. We had to find out if she would be able to get back into Westmont. I had talked with Westmont the week before on another matter and, in the course of the conversation, was told that there was a waiting list for students wanting to enroll in Westmont. Had one of these students already been given her spot? As soon as the Admissions Office opened on Tuesday morning, Sarah was on the telephone. She talked with the admissions director and asked if it was possible for her to come back, and he said he would do what he could and would call right back. We waited until 7 p.m. that night for him to call. He had to do a lot of groundwork to make it happen, but he did it! SHE WAS IN! And not only that, she would even have her same room back with her same roommates.

3. The restaurant management was very gracious and said they would hold the job for her until summer.

4. The weight-loss clinic agreed to refund her money.

5. Her Minneapolis physician had an appointment open later that very morning and would take off the mole.

6. After the admissions director's call came in at 7 p.m., Rich and I were at the mall before they closed at 9 p.m. to get an airline ticket for Sarah, and she was scheduled to be on the plane at 5 a.m. the next morning, returning to Santa Barbara to complete her junior year.

7. Sarah called several of her professors and was read-mitted into all the classes she had originally registered for. When she returned to Westmont the next day, she would have only missed one day of classes.

8. The situation with Sarah's dorm room at Westmont was truly another "special touch" of God in Sarah's life...another "small" miracle! But, no touch of God is small. This was huge in our minds! As I mentioned earlier, Sarah was assigned the very same room she had just left, and of course with the same roommates. But what we did not know at the time was "the rest of the story." Once Sarah was back in her dorm, her roommates told her the most amazing story. After Sarah left, the room was available and therefore was assigned to another roommate. That student ended up not coming to Westmont, which

left the room available again. The roommates then went to Housing to request that one of their friends be allowed to move into that room. To their surprise, their request was denied because there was a "hold" on that room; it was being held for someone else. They wondered for whom, but were not told. In fact, the hold could not have been for Sarah because the roommates' request had taken place two days before Sarah actually called to get back in to Westmont. However, when Sarah called, the college assigned her to that very dorm room again. The roommates all were stunned and, I am confident, also knew it was a "touch" of God!

Thank you...thank you...thank you, God!

Chapter 12

"I DIDN'T WANT ANY PART OF YOU OR YOUR GOD!"

*"Halleluiah! Thank you, Lord...Who can
ever list the glorious miracles of God? Who can
ever praise Him half enough?"*
Psalms 106:1–2

*S*arah was very grateful to be back at Westmont to complete her junior year of college. We were also grateful to have her in this faith environment where she was growing close to many friends and to God. She would often call home and tell me about something she had heard in chapel that day that had impacted her, or to suggest a book written by the chapel speaker that had touched her. After those conversations, my prayers were always of thanksgiving! I knew that God had touched her life in a mighty way, but I did not know how deeply until I got the following letter from her. You need to know that I have retyped it for this reading, because, as you must know by now, anyone reading her writing more than likely would not be able to decipher it because of her writing disability. The words, however, are truly her own.

Dear Mom,

I just got back from a "yucky" history test; think I might have failed it. And then I stopped at my mailbox and found your letter. I decided, Mom, I just have to tell you how much I appreciate the things you say in your letters, like today after the test. I just needed to hear you say, "Keep your eyes on Jesus!" That made me remember just how much He cares what happens to me. And as long as I keep my thoughts on Him (like you keep reminding me), even if I fail my test, He is still right beside me. And boy, do I really need Him right beside me this week!

You'll probably want to sit down now, Mom, but I got to thinking that I have never really told you, after all these years, how much of my life is really centered in Jesus. Do you remember how I used to fight it? All the troubles I was having, there was no way that I could see how God could really care about me!

But, looking back now, I guess it was because you never got shook and always insisted that God loved me and cared for me, and even though I ranted and raved, deep down I knew that I wanted the God that you always talked about.

I remember several different times when I was sick and we didn't know exactly what was wrong. You would sit on the floor by me while I was lying on the sofa, and you would read from your favorite book about how much God cared for me and loved me and that, if I kept my mind on God, there would be no room in my mind for thinking about scary things and about what was wrong with me. I never told you then, maybe I didn't really even know, but I know I somehow felt better inside even though I didn't really know why.

I remember how you kept wanting to have family devotions, and I was always in a hurry to go someplace or too tired. Then you and Dad decided to wake me at 6:15 in the morning. You both sat on my bedroom floor, and I had to at least sit up in bed. We all had our Bibles and those silly yellow marking pens, and we had to mark the places that you thought we would want to remember and find easily sometime later; all I wanted to do was either sleep some more or get going because I might be late for school. You promised me that we would take only as long as I had time for—maybe fifteen minutes, maybe just five minutes, and some mornings all we had time for was a prayer. I probably will never forget the morning you shared with us, before your minor surgery, verses that kept you from being worried or frightened. In fact, I often now find those verses marked in yellow in my Bible when I need to feel Jesus close to me. Can you believe that? Did you think you would ever hear me say that?

Do you remember the night that I had really had it? It was a terrible day, it had been a terrible week—in fact, life was terrible—and I just knew that things would never get any better! I told you I was giving up, I was too tired to keep going; my body and brain were too tired. I knew that I was only kidding myself, that I could really do it. You tried to tell me about some verses in the Bible that would make me feel better, and I remember I was SO down and SO depressed. I looked at you and said with every bone in my body, **"Do you really believe that stuff? What for? Nothing ever happens for me, nothing ever changes!"** *I remember yelling that at you and running upstairs to my bedroom, where I shut the door and cried myself to sleep.* **I didn't want any part of you or your God!**

But then, Mom, I want to tell you something that I'm sure you don't know. You thought I was asleep when you came into my bedroom later that night. I had been asleep, but I woke up and knew you were sitting on my bed. I heard you reading the Bible very quietly. I really didn't know what it was you were reading—I bet it was some of the promises you always tell me about, wasn't it? You have always told me that the Bible is full of promises that God has made to me, and that He always keeps them. Then, Mom, I heard you slip off the bed and kneel by my bed. I'm not sure how long you were there, because then I did fall back asleep. Mom, I've known many other nights when you were kneeling by my bed. You remember, Mom, that I didn't wake up the next morning a new person. (God doesn't always work that way, does He?) In fact, you could hardly get me up the next morning—but soon after I again picked myself up, became strong, and went on. And now I know, Mom, that God answered your prayers and kept His promises to me—maybe not just the way I (or you) wanted them to be answered, and certainly not always in the time we wanted, but He always was there for me, keeping His promises and loving me just the way I was, even with my ugly disposition and crankiness and temper.

My struggles never ended, as you well know, and many, many times I still get really, really down; but it seems that as I continued to struggle, I began to feel that God was with me in my struggles, and little by little I began to feel closer and closer to Him.

You know that I am still struggling—college is SO hard! I have a hard time reading my textbooks; it's hard for me to stay at studying; I don't always understand the test questions; I need help writing my papers—and then if all of that wasn't bad enough, the first eighteen months of college I felt like a medical case study. There was therapy on my knee for three months (almost needed surgery), that lump on my back that the doctors didn't know what it was and I finally had to have minor surgery to remove it, then there was the ovarian cyst and all the x-rays, the mole that was doing funny things, and then I was scheduled for surgery, minor toe surgery (caused by my hiking boots), discovered another lump in my back—it just seemed to go on and on and on.

Remember, Mom, how you would always remind me over and over again that Jesus held me in the palm of His hand? I always thought you were really ridiculous—but you know, Mom, if I didn't have all those things to cling to, I know I never would have made it! You kept telling me that I was a child of God and there was nothing that I could ever do that could make God stop loving me. Mom, don't ever stop telling me that! I feel so close to Him now, and I know that He loves me and will never leave me no matter where I am or what I do.

Can you believe it, Mom? Can you believe that I am really telling you all of this? And, Mom, don't ever stop praying for me!

There were no words to convey my overwhelming feelings when I finished reading Sarah's powerful letter! Only to fall on my knees in adoration and thanksgiving to our unfailing God!

GREAT IS HIS FAITHFULNESS!

It was also during these Westmont years that Sarah began to share many other personal feelings. She would often send cards, such as "Thanks, Mom, for being there when I need you!" Or this one: "Thank you for your quiet strength and gentle understanding. Though I know I don't tell you often enough, I think you know how much you mean to me—for what would I be without your guidance in my life? I love you, Mom!" And this was written in a card: "Thank you so much for all you do for me. I couldn't make it without you and your constant support." I loved getting these cards: "The Best Thing To Do In A Crisis Is Call Your Mom!" and "Thanks Mom For Loving Me Even When I Had My Pouty Face On."

Sarah sent me several small books over the years, such as *Why a Daughter Needs a Mom* and *I'm Happy when You're Happy*. I've gotten meaningful little trinkets from Sarah: among my favorites are two pink purses, one stating "Like Mother" and the other "Like Daughter," and both purses have cell phones peeking out! And I love this small wall hanging: "Life began with waking up and loving my Mother's face" (George Eliot). I also have several coffee cups from Sarah that are really special: one says "Home is where your Mom is" and another "Call your Mom." My very favorite, which I look at every day when I am working in my office, says "Mother-Daughter" on the front, and on the back, "Mother, our relationship is special to me, and I thank you for all you are to my life…my Mother, my Friend, My Guide." The inside of the cup tells me, "The bonds we have are everlasting!" I have a T-shirt from Sarah that reads: "Mother's Day every day" and another: "I Love Mom." What a treasure! Sarah was, and still is, so faithful to always stay in touch!

Thank you…thank you…thank you, God!

Chapter 13

"LORD, KEEP ME CALM AND GIVE ME DIRECTION!"

"But, oh, the joys of those who put their TRUST in Him."
Psalms 2:12b

*S*arah's faith continued to grow, even as she was struggling. And she did continue to struggle...and struggle. She was so grateful to be back at Westmont and for the opportunity to "try again." And yet, as one can imagine, school did not get any easier.

Even the fun and relaxing times with her friends were laden with those familiar, tough questions: *What about the coming year? Where should I really be going? Should I stay here and continue to struggle, or should I be looking at something else? How long can I really endure this painful struggle? Augsburg College back in Minneapolis offers a program for students with learning disabilities; should I be considering this for my senior year?* Her mind was constantly processing all the options.

Sarah did complete her junior year at Westmont. She spent the summer in Santa Barbara living with friends and working at a small gift shop there. She loved just "living" in Santa Barbara without any stress. But as the summer wore on, she knew she had to make another major decision and again address the inevitable question—what should she do in the fall? Westmont or Augsburg? I vividly remember our telephone conversation during this struggle. Rich and I were on vacation with friends in Yosemite that July. She called us and shared her familiar struggle over what to do. I finally made the suggestion that when we arrived back home we would buy a plane ticket for her to come home for a week to at least do the testing for Augsburg. Relieved to have someone else make the decision for her, she agreed to do as we suggested. Sarah came home for one week during the end of July.

Elayne, Sarah's tutor, had always been included in important decisions as a mentor and advisor. She would be instrumental in facilitating this next decision as well. Sarah contacted Augsburg and was advised that, to enroll in their program for students with learning disabilities, she would need additional testing. Elayne, however, was not qualified to administer all of the testing required by Augsburg. Instead, she referred Sarah to Brian, an educational psychologist, for the additional testing needed.

Sarah came home on Friday, spent time with her friends over the weekend, and met with Elayne on Monday. Elayne had scheduled Sarah an appointment with Brian on Tuesday afternoon. Sarah went to this appointment alone and was on her way home when the telephone rang at our home. It was Brian. This had been a routine testing appointment, so I certainly was not expecting any alarming news. However, during the conversation with Brian, it became alarming. The routine testing for a college application had, in fact, revealed some important results he wanted to share with us. Sarah's testing indicated a slight depression which he felt we should be aware of immediately. His recommendation was for Sarah to see a counselor.

Okay, God, keep me calm and give me direction! God heard my prayer and did just that. Sarah walked in shortly after I hung up the phone, and I shared with her my conversation with Brian. She did not seem to be shaken by this at all, so I told her I would call someone first thing in the morning for an appointment. I was on my knees again that night to ask God for wisdom and direction as we made the next decision. I had no idea who to call, but I did remember a friend mentioning the name of a doctor in practice at a Christian counseling center near us. First thing the next morning, I was on the phone with the counseling center. The doctor I asked about did not have an opening that day, but they were able to refer me to a doctor in another practice. I immediately called his office and scheduled an appointment for that afternoon. Less than twenty-four hours since the call from Brian, we were in that doctor's office.

Thank you...thank you...thank you, God!

One may wonder what Sarah's reaction was to all of this.

She was unbelievably calm, accepting, unquestioning, and eager to move on. Our appointment with the doctor was in the late afternoon; apparently it was his last appointment for the day because he was in no hurry to end our conversation. Sarah visited with him for about an hour before I was called in. To our amazement, and I think also to his, after an hour with Sarah this doctor was fairly convinced that she had the same symptoms he himself had! These were not symptoms of actual depression, as we know it, but of a chemical imbalance in the brain. He described it, in part, as the brain not focusing and being "too hyper." He was eager to give us the name of the doctor who was treating him—Dr. Faruk Abuzzahab, a very well-respected psychopharmacologist in this seven-state area. He was in private practice but has also been on the faculty of the University of Minnesota for thirty years.

The very next morning we were in Dr. Abuzzahab's office for our first appointment. After all, we had to move quickly because Sarah had only one day left before returning to Santa Barbara. At this first appointment, there was no way to know what this man would eventually mean to Sarah's life and to her future. To this day, we continue to thank God for bringing Dr. Faruk Abuzzahab into Sarah's life!

After talking with Sarah for about an hour, this kind man came into the waiting room and beckoned me into his office. His gentleness and personal touch have been consistent at every visit with him. He was never in a hurry and always spent as much time as needed to answer all our questions and concerns. At this initial visit, after only an hour with Sarah, he had a diagnosis and a treatment plan, which has not changed in twenty-three years!

His diagnosis was that Sarah has a chemical imbalance related to her learning disabilities. There is a high correlation between biochemical depression (caused by a neurotransmitter dysfunction in the brain) and learning disabilities. Chemical imbalance is often the general term for depression—Brian was right! The connection between dyslexia and brain chemistry was just beginning to be researched and recognized. Dr. Abuzzahab's field of psychopharmacology helped him make the correct diagnosis and recognize all the components. Sarah also had a thyroid imbalance, which often accompanies dyslexia. And it was with his expertise that we began to recognize that Sarah also had symptoms of attention deficit disorder (ADD), which is associated with dyslexia as well. I knew immediately it was God that connected us to these two doctors!

Thank you...thank you...thank you, God!

We were quickly learning so many new terms related to Sarah's diagnosis. One of them was ADD: attention deficit disorder; or in some cases ADHD: attention deficit hyperactivity disorder. Actually, Sarah could technically be considered attention deficit hyperactivity disorder (ADHD) because, as Dr. Abuzzahab explained to us, although Sarah was not hyperactive physically, her brain was hyperactive.

We accepted all of this with confidence and peace, because we immediately recognized and trusted that we were in the hands of an expert.

Before we left the appointment, Dr. Abuzzahab explained in detail his long-range treatment plan for Sarah. He immediately prescribed an over-the-counter drug for her: L-tyrosine, a natural amino acid that is converted in the brain to dopamine, which calms a hyperactive brain. With a hyperactive brain, he said, it would be extremely difficult to concentrate and focus, and therefore would certainly interfere with any learning process. Wow...did this ever open our eyes. No wonder she had difficulty in school! She was to start with this drug and then, at her next appointments, he would begin the process of adding other appropriate prescription medications. He discouraged Sarah from returning to Westmont. Instead, he encouraged her to begin this treatment plan immediately, which would mean regular weekly appointments in Minneapolis.

Sarah and I left that appointment pretty overwhelmed, yet so incredibly relieved and excited that somebody had identified what she was actually going through and, most importantly, had an answer! We both felt so good about Dr. Abuzzahab and trusted him and his diagnosis. We only found out later what "trusting him" would really mean.

Sarah was so glad to have a label for what she had—generally termed depression. And not only that, she was excited to tell others what she had. Wouldn't this help them understand, too? Well, that excitement didn't last very long. She immediately began telling her friends that she had depression. But, she was very puzzled. Whenever she told anyone about the depression, they seemed to become quiet and act a little differently toward her. You see, the general population has a very different impression of what depression actually is. And, of course, most people automatically think of clinical depression being associated with the diagnosis of a chemical imbalance in the brain. It just happens that brain chemical imbalances include dyslexia as well.

I spent the next months reading and researching everything I could get my hands on regarding the diagnosis of brain chemical imbalance as related to dyslexia. I spent hours at the University of Minnesota library reading whatever literature there was; in 1989 there was not a lot of information on dyslexia and the chemistry of the brain. In my ongoing research, I was able to learn, recognize, and accept all of the manifestations of this learning disability.

I was very grateful for everything I learned, because I felt I was at least beginning to understand Sarah and her struggles. When I look back at her years of struggling, with the knowledge that I have now, I am absolutely amazed and overwhelmed that she survived and remained the happy, peaceful person she was. We later learned she probably was not *always* that happy, peaceful person on the *inside*. I thanked God again and again for holding her in His hands all those years and helping her to maintain balance in everything she did, and to achieve a measure of success in so many areas of her life.

Chapter 14

"IF YOU DON'T DISCONTINUE THIS MEDICATION, YOU WILL NOT LIVE TO BE TWENTY-SEVEN YEARS OLD!"

"I want you to trust me in your time of trial...so I can rescue you...and you can give me glory!" Psalms 50:15

*S*arah accepted Dr. Abuzzahab's recommendation to stay in Minneapolis. Instead of returning for school, she returned to Santa Barbara to collect all of her things, quit her job, and move out of the apartment with her friends. This process was another sad experience for her, but she knew she was, once again, beginning another new chapter in her life. In the fall of 1989, she moved into an apartment with two friends in Minneapolis and began her senior year at Augsburg College. She was accepted into the program for students with learning disabilities at Augsburg with the hopes of getting additional help with her classes, but this program was not as beneficial as we had hoped. She continued to struggle in each class and with each assignment. We both would stay up late at night while she was writing a paper. I was trying to help her organize her thoughts without actually dictating the paper.

Discouragement continued to prevail until I was led to a new thought. In all my research into dyslexia, I found that it was considered very, very helpful for dyslexics to have a professional "coach" to meet with on a regular basis. I found myself actively networking once again, this time to find a coach for Sarah. I finally found Miriam, a coach who was there for Sarah as a mentor and support. Sarah recognized that her regular appointments with Miriam were proving to be one of the most helpful interventions during this chapter in her life. We were also connected with another educational specialist, Joanne, who met with Sarah to do more testing and was also a wonderful support for her.

After Sarah had settled again in Minnesota, she was excited to get back to her appointments with Dr. Abuzzahab and begin her treatment program. Sarah and I spent a number of appointments with Dr. Abuzzahab that fall. Not only was his diagnosis flawless, but his treatment included regular diagnostic blood testing to make certain the drugs he was prescribing were actually performing in Sarah's body the way he intended. He made it very clear to us that each body can metabolize drugs differently, so this blood testing was a consistent procedure of his during the treatment. His treatment plan was initiated after talking with Sarah and analyzing blood work. He wrote out three prescriptions for her: Wellbutrin (which was still new in the field), to treat the chemical imbalance of dyslexia; Cylert, which was a prescription for calming the brain (this took the place of the over-the-counter drug, L-tyrosine); and Synthroid, for treating her thyroid imbalance. He prescribed these three drugs during her first appointments and although he later took Sarah off of the Cylert (which was taken off the market due to liver toxicity in children), he has never changed anything else except the dosage in the twenty-three years since then. To this day, Sarah is still on the same medications—Wellbutrin and Synthroid—that Dr. Abuzzahab prescribed from the very beginning. Many times he would tell us, "I know what I am doing. Just trust me." And we did!

Dr. Abuzzahab spent a number of months adjusting the dosages of Sarah's medications and doing blood work to check on how her body was metabolizing the drugs. He did tell us that she may experience side effects as he was changing the dosage of the medications. And she did. She was one of the rare individuals who experienced almost every side effect one could have. Knowing our trust in him was tested during these times, Dr. Abuzzahab reminded us that he was well aware of the side effects and they would not last long. He encouraged us not to be concerned, and we tried our best not to be.

During these months of adjusting the medications, Sarah moved home—to our sofa! She spent many days on that sofa riding through the side effects. Wellbutrin was the medication the doctor continued to adjust as he was monitoring how it was being metabolized in her body. Each time she went back for an appointment, he would increase the dosage of the Wellbutrin, because her body was, in fact, metabolizing the drug. For her body, the dosage had to be very high in order for the medication to metabolize and be effective. In fact, as he was beginning to increase it, he also prescribed an anti-seizure drug as a safeguard until her body adjusted to the drug. Thankfully, this risk did not become a problem.

Each episode of a side effect would only last for a short time and then would never return again. As time went on, we became used to the progression of side effects, because each one would happen exactly as Dr. Abuzzahab predicted and then be gone. As he carefully monitored changes in medications, he continued to ask us to trust him. And we did!

One side effect did become somewhat alarming. During the first few weeks of being on the anti-seizure drug, Sarah actually became obsessive-compulsive, a known side effect of this drug. We were not at all familiar with Obsessive-Compulsive Disorder (OCD), so we understandably became a little alarmed with this behavior. But we continued to trust Dr. Abuzzahab as we watched all this happen. OCD manifested itself in a number of different ways in Sarah's life. Some of the behaviors were very much out of character for her. For instance, all of her clothes had to be folded just right, she felt the need to clean the funniest spots in the house, and she exhibited other obsessive behaviors. Because her body became pretty exhausted and weary, she spent a lot of time on the sofa watching TV. However, she also became interested in many, many things that would never have appealed to her before. For instance, she was fascinated by what her Dad was doing at work. She also took a new interest in the news and what was happening locally and nationally. During all of this we kept our eyes on Dr. Abuzzahab, who continued to say, "Trust me!" And, of course, as we were keeping our eyes on Dr. Abuzzahab, I daily left her in God's hands, who also said, "Trust Me!" And we did! Sarah's OCD behavior did not last more than a month, and then, as Dr. Abuzzahab predicted, it disappeared.

Sarah finished her first semester of her senior year at Augsburg College, but then made another major decision. She decided, once again, to move back to Santa Barbara, but this time just to work and not go to school. In January, she rented an apartment with a college friend and found a job. Her final semester of college would be put on hold for the time being.

Sarah enjoyed her job and, of course, was *so* thrilled to be back in California, so I didn't expect another anxious phone call. Therefore, I was surprised one day when I received a distraught phone call. She was having frightening heart palpitations. Rich and I assumed that they could be another side effect of the medication, but we wanted to confirm our suspicions. We advised Sarah to see a doctor in Santa Barbara.

Sarah visited the doctor she had seen before, and he was extremely alarmed by the dosage of the medication she was taking. Sitting in his office, Sarah was already apprehensive when he told her, "If you don't discontinue this medication, you will not live to be twenty-seven years old." At this time, Sarah was twenty-one. He continued, "I can no longer keep you as a patient if you don't stop the medication, because I won't know what to tell the medical board when you die!"

As soon as Sarah returned to her apartment she called me, understandably shaken about this doctor's proclamation. I was startled as well. I assured Sarah that I would be calling Dr. Abuzzahab first thing in the morning and would call her immediately after. The doctor's office opened at 8 a.m. in the morning, and it couldn't come soon enough. When I told him the exact words of the Santa Barbara doctor, it took him only about ninety seconds to relieve my mind. "Yes, this is a side effect, but no, it is not serious and it will not last long. And please, trust me!" I hung up the phone, was at peace, put my "blinders" on, kept my eyes on Dr. Abuzzahab, and trusted him! From that day forward, we looked neither right nor left, but only straight ahead to Dr. Abuzzahab. We have never wavered since, and he has never let us down!

Twenty-two years later, extremely healthy at the age of forty-four, Sarah is still taking the medication and wouldn't choose to live without it! The heart palpitations lasted only a few days longer, and she has never had them since.

Sarah eventually visited another doctor affiliated with the Los Angeles medical school. He happened to know of Dr. Abuzzahab and his reputation. He told her, "Dr. Abuzzahab knows what he is doing, and whatever he advises and prescribes will be the right thing." This was extremely comforting to all of us.

Thank you...thank you...thank you, God!

Chapter 15

"AND *HOW* MUCH DOES IT COST?"

"The Lord will work out His plans for my life."
Psalms 138:8a

*I*t was now May in Santa Barbara. Sarah's life was less stressful: no school, just working and "hanging out" with friends, and she was feeling good because of her medications. Life was less stressful, but not exactly peaceful. During all her years of struggling with her learning disabilities, she was very aware of how they interfered with what she wanted to do with her life. It wasn't until much later that I *really* realized what was going on internally with Sarah or *really* understood how she had to wake up to wrestle with her disabilities each and every day. Consciously or unconsciously, she was always "searching."

While at Westmont, she was introduced to a support group for adults with dyslexia. She had attended several of their meetings while in school and stayed in contact with the group when she was in Santa Barbara. At one of the meetings she heard about a conference on dyslexia in

Los Angeles. She attended this weekend conference and was very motivated by one of the speakers, Dr. Larry Silver. It was during this weekend that I received a very exciting telephone call: "Mom, I just heard about a school in Vermont for dyslexics. They have a summer program starting in June. Do you think I could go?"

She proceeded to tell me how excited she was about everything she heard at the conference. More importantly, the door was opened into a whole new world of possibilities—there really were other people out there with a disability like hers. Not only that, this school in Vermont claimed to be able to make a difference in their lives. I had never heard her so emotional and so connected to her disability. Something significant had happened to her that weekend.

Many thoughts raced through my mind: *There really is a school for dyslexics? Wow…why wouldn't we send her there? She is interested in pursuing this? She must really be feeling hopeful! Another move…again! And, how much does it cost?*

Of course we wanted to know more about this amazing place. I told her on the phone that after Dad and I received a little more information, we would think about it and let her know our decision. I think she was a little surprised that we were willing to even consider it (she probably already *knew* the cost of the program). She came away from the conference with a lot of information about Landmark College in Putney, Vermont.

Landmark College was founded in 1985 as the first college in the world exclusively for students with learning disabilities and, in particular, dyslexia. Because of the specialized focus of the college, individuals of all ages and from all over the world attended Landmark. I contacted the school for more information about the summer program... and the *cost!* My heart was so broken at this time, and I felt so deeply the anguish Sarah had been going through all these years, anything that would give her some hope for a meaningful future was shouting at me: "Do it for her...and *forget the cost!*"

What I learned about the summer program, and Landmark College in general, was absolutely overwhelming. Was there really something out there that would enable my daughter to live a "normal" life? And why wouldn't we provide that for her? My simple prayer for Sarah had always been only that she be able to *function* out there in life, in the real world. That is all I had been asking of God. And so I again fell on my knees immediately to ask for God's guidance and direction: *Should we spend the money for this summer program at Landmark College?* Rich and I had wrestled and wrestled with this question ever since the telephone call. We finally decided to go to bed and address it the next morning. To my amazement, Rich got up the next morning and said (even after hearing the cost), "It seems to be the right thing; let's do it."

Now that I had Rich's okay, I needed to get God's okay! After much time on my knees and quiet time with God, I was at peace with the plan to send Sarah to Landmark College for the summer program. She was thrilled with our decision, and I immediately called Landmark to apply for the summer program. I took on another bookkeeping job, and we were able to pay the $7,000 for the five-week summer program.

Sarah did, however, have to visit Landmark before being accepted for the program. Since the summer program was beginning in several weeks, she would have to visit there immediately. She was planning to fly home on Thursday from California; on Saturday she would continue on to Vermont for her interview. But after thinking and praying about this, I felt I should drive with her and visit the school as well. However, it was important to me to have Rich's support. I had approached him with this idea just the day before Sarah came home, and he thought it was a good idea. Keep in mind, this is a little outside his character, as it was both last-minute and money spent. I was terribly relieved and very thankful for this blessing!

We picked Sarah up at the airport on Thursday afternoon, and I told her we would be driving together to Vermont the next morning. I had no time to visit AAA for driving maps or directions, but we knew where we were headed and what cities we would be traveling through. We decided that we would simply get into the car and follow the green highway signs for the next city, and it worked. We arrived on Sunday afternoon at an inn in Putney, Vermont, for our Monday morning appointment with the Landmark College admissions director, Carolyn Olivier.

Chapter 16

"SHE WILL NEED TO BE HERE FOR THREE TO FOUR YEARS."

"Thou wilt keep him in perfect peace whose mind is stayed on Thee." Isaiah 26:3 (KJV)

We arrived at Carolyn Olivier's office, and Sarah was not nervous at all. I was, but not Sarah! While waiting, I visited with a young man who was also there for his appointment. I could easily see that he was *very* nervous. I began chatting with him, and he told me he was also from Minnesota: from Rochester, home of the Mayo Clinic. His parents were both doctors at Mayo. I was a little surprised that he was so nervous and Sarah was not. After her interview, Sarah confirmed that she had not been nervous at all. I concluded that she could visit with the President of the United States and not be nervous! Ever since, I am continually amazed at her composure when talking with people. I am not at all sure where she gets her confidence, but it truly is a blessing for her.

Mrs. Olivier called us both into her office for a

post-interview conversation. We visited briefly, and then Mrs. Olivier asked me to read a paper out loud that Sarah had written for her during the interview. I was not at all prepared for the "weirdness" of this paper. *Where, oh where, did this strange flow of ideas come from?* The paper truly made *no sense* at all! Following is Sarah's entry into her journal referencing this interview and paper:

> I remember getting my first computer when I was at Westmont. I plugged it in and typed my first paper. I thought, *This is what I've needed all these years. Type my paper, hit "Spell Check," and,* voila!, *I'm Einstein!* I thought to myself, *I will go places, I've got a computer.* However, my Communication teacher didn't think I was Einstein, or even close to it, for that matter. He read the first paragraph, marked it up with a thick red pen, and handed it back to me. He said he couldn't go on because there were no complete sentences, there were misused words, there were spelling errors, and, most of all, it didn't make sense. So my "Einstein image" was shattered in a matter of days. My computer purchase was just another cruel tease in the hope of finding a cure for my learning problems.
>
> When I heard about Landmark College, I just knew that I needed to check it out. I'll

never forget the first time I visited Landmark. I was interviewed, tested, and photographed. During the testing section, I was trying to break the ice by being funny, only to find out that the person administrating the test was the school "shrink"! I thought, *GREAT! All my comments, jokes, and stories* (which were probably pretty random, considering I was in a new surrounding and I was being asked questions such as, "How would you get out of the forest if you were lost?" and "Who was Winnie the Pooh's friend?") *are being analyzed!*

I was then asked to write a paragraph about horses. I'm thinking, *No problem, I've had three and a half years of college. I've written essays, short stories, and theory papers.* (Okay, I must confess—in college I faxed my ideas, which I called a rough draft, back to my tutor in Minneapolis, and she corrected them and faxed them back. Basically, I wrote the papers, or at least the ideas were mine. With this perfected system, I felt college could be a breeze!)

After my test I talked to Mrs. Olivier, and she asked me to read the paragraph I had written about horses. I thought I'd fly through this. I'm a Speech Communication major. I read my paragraph with such ease and confidence. For some reason, she asked me to read it again, and once again I read it with ease. Then she asked me to read it for a third time. This got me thinking: *Reading the same paragraph about horses three times isn't a regular interview procedure.* However, I read it once again. After this, Mrs. Olivier said she wanted to read it out loud to me. Mrs. Olivier's version was completely different than mine! Her version went something like this: "The horse brown stands beautiful and strong sometimes carrying people showing running jumping fast high leaping." My reaction was, "What gives! Where'd you come up with that?" Unfortunately, she had a witness— my mother. Mrs. Olivier had my mother read it, and she came up with the same version. For the first time I realized I *really* need help! I'm twenty-three years old, and I can't even write a paragraph on horses! I'll never forget when Mrs. Olivier said to my mother, "She'll need to be here at least three to four years." And I'll never forget my mother's reply: "And *HOW* much is tuition again?" From that moment on my life changed completely!

As Sarah's mother sitting there in that office reading the alarming and confusing paper about horses, my stunned reaction truly *was*, "And *HOW* much is tuition again?" Mrs. Olivier also told us that, after analyzing Sarah's testing, she was reading at the second-grade level, and she confirmed that Sarah would have to be at Landmark for at least three or four years. She also told me that during the testing process, Sarah had to be given the reading test a second time, verbally, because her score on the first test was so unbelievably low. Because of her low scores she was enrolled in the lowest reading and writing classes and was unable to receive college credit for her classes.

At that point in our lives, the tuition at Landmark College was beyond our comprehension, but we were told there would be financial aid available. We were advised in great detail how we could apply for a scholarship at Landmark, and we were also given information about applying for financial aid and student loans. Because they believed so strongly that they could make a difference in Sarah's life, they wanted to help us in any way they could. Looking back on our journey, we can say with confidence that, yes, they did—they made a *huge difference* in Sarah's life!

Three important forces combined and changed Sarah's life. Sarah is what she is today in large part because of Landmark College. But, she also is what she is today because of Dr. Abuzzahab! If it was not for his wise evaluation and skill in prescribing medication, she would have been unable to concentrate, focus, and be productive at Landmark. Sarah's tutor, Elayne, was invaluable in her life. Not only did she help Sarah academically, but she became a mentor/friend, giving her self-confidence and encouragement in each step of her way.

However, Sarah *really* is what she is today because of God's guidance and direction all along her journey. He brought just the right people and places into her life at just the right times: Minnehaha Academy, Cookie and Elayne, Miriam, Joanne, Westmont College, Brian, Dr. V, Dr. Abuzzahab, and Landmark College. God truly was there with her each step of the way!

Thank you...thank you...thank you, God!

Once we returned home, I took on more bookkeeping jobs and Sarah returned to Landmark College for the summer program. I felt at peace that we were truly leaving the choice to Him, and as Jim Elliot once said, "God gives His best to those who leave the choice to Him."

Chapter 17

"YOU DON'T WANT TO
GO TO MACYS?"

*"Oh give thanks to the Lord...who alone does
great wonders!"* Psalms 136:4

he five weeks that Sarah spent in the summer program at Landmark College proved to be an incred-
ible turning point in her life. After going to college for three
and a half years, Sarah still could not either read a complete
book or write a paper that made any sense at all. How could
five weeks in *any* program change this? I have no answer to
this question except to "shout from the mountain top": IT DID!

After only five weeks at Landmark, Sarah's reading, her
interest in reading, and her writing were so miraculously
changed that it brought me to my knees with tears. I did not
understand what had happened and I did not question it. I only
thanked God for this miracle in Sarah's life!

Thank you...thank you...thank you, God!

She came home after the summer and immediately wanted to go shopping. So what else is new? Sarah LOVED shopping! We went to the mall, but to my surprise, instead of going to her favorite department store for the newest sweater or jeans, she headed right for Barnes and Noble. *Wait...Barnes and Noble? That's a* book *store!* I'm not sure how long we stayed, but I do know that Sarah did not want to leave. I went browsing myself and when ready to leave, where did I find her? She wasn't in the fiction or aerobics or cooking section, but in the *psychology* section! She was totally captivated by books on the brain, genetics, psychology, and dyslexia.

Can you even believe that this young adult, who at age twenty-two was reading at a second-grade level, had **never** read a full book, did not **want** to read a book, and actually **couldn't** read a book, was in Barnes and Noble totally absorbed in *books*!

Not only had Sarah developed a love for reading, but her writing had improved dramatically as well. I thought back on the professor telling her that he couldn't make sense of her papers. I also remembered Sarah's paper that I had read aloud in the Admissions Office at Landmark College, which made absolutely no sense at all. This was our second miracle: after five weeks at Landmark, she was writing papers that made sense!

Sarah spent the rest of the summer waitressing and was actually able to buy a small white used Volkswagen Beetle. We had already made the decision that Sarah would spend the next year at Landmark, so now she would be able to drive herself to Vermont for the fall semester. Because we had family living in Chicago, I drove there with her on her way to Vermont. I will never forget the morning when she left Chicago. It was about 6:30 a.m. when I followed her little Beetle to the entrance of the freeway. My heart was heavy, scared, and excited all at the same time as I watched that little white car move up the ramp onto the freeway. I watched until I could no longer see her. She was on her way alone many miles to Putney, Vermont, to continue down this wonderful path that God had set her on.

Chapter 18

"RICH! LOOK WHAT JUST CAME IN THE MAIL!"

"And my God shall supply all your need according to His riches in glory by Christ Jesus." Philippians 4:19 (KJV)

*L*andmark College was an absolutely amazing place of learning. Sarah became friends with students of all ages from all across the U.S. and the world. There were students from a broad spectrum of backgrounds; some much like her and other students with very well-known parents. Because they all came from years and years of struggling with learning disabilities, they all developed a very special bond. The professors were outstanding in their fields, as well as in relating to the students. The professor/student ratio was approximately five students to one professor. It was common for each student to have three to four classes each day. Every day the professors of each of these classes would meet to coordinate the learning for each individual student. Sarah thrived in this learning environment. She bonded with students and professors alike in this small setting. Many of the friends she made at Landmark are her friends still.

As you can imagine, a specialized learning environment like the one provided at Landmark comes with a price tag. I, of course, was well aware of this the first time I visited the campus. By this time, we were well past the "sticker shock" and were determined to find a way to keep Sarah there. I took on more accounting jobs, and we watched our budget very carefully. The sacrifice was worth it, and we were extremely grateful for this opportunity in Sarah's life. We had identified a number of sources of financial aid, but by the end of the first semester we were still struggling to meet our next payment. We were faced with the reality that our next payment was due by the first of the year, and we were about $3,000 short! On my knees, I left this too in God's hands. I was strengthened again by His reminder to trust Him; He assured me that nothing is too big for Him to handle.

It was just a few days before Christmas when I opened the mail, and to my overwhelming surprise, out fell a cashier's check for $3,000! I looked for the name of our benefactor, but the check was totally anonymous. Tears flowed and I knelt at my bed, thanking God for this overwhelming miracle.

To this day, we have not discovered who sent the check. All we know is that it was an amazing sign of God's touch! *We* do not know who, but *God* does. We remember this in our daily prayers and ask God to mightily bless the donor(s).

Thank you…thank you…thank you, God!

Chapter 19

"THY NAME IS COURAGE"

"But those who trust in the Lord shall renew their strength; they shall mount up with wings like eagles; they shall run and not be weary; they shall walk and not faint."
Isaiah 40:13

ich and I visited the campus of Landmark College for Parent's Weekend in the fall of 1991 and were so very impressed with the staff, students, and environment. You may have noticed I have not used the word "stressed" in the last couple of chapters. What an absolute blessing that time was…Sarah truly had not been stressed at Landmark. This time, after I sent her off to school, I never answered the telephone and heard, "I'm stressed and I want to come home!" What an answer to another prayer; each of Sarah's needs were being met at Landmark College. She was learning; she was successful; she was happy; and she was with people who truly "understood her."

Thank you…thank you…thank you, God!

For the rest of our lives we will be thankful to Landmark College for four major accomplishments in Sarah's life:

1. She learned in-depth about her disability, her strengths, and her weaknesses, and most importantly, to feel good about herself.

2. She learned to read! Not only could Sarah not read, but she was never in the least *interested* in reading. Now I can hardly get her to leave a bookstore, she carries a paperback book in her bag, and it's not unusual to hear her say to me, "Don't bother me, I'm reading!"

3. She learned to write. After the summer program, I told Rich that the five papers she wrote during that summer were worth all the money we spent for the entire program. Her Landmark teachers told us that she is a very creative thinker and writer; that she always had it in her, but was never able to "get it out."

4. She learned to be comfortable speaking in public. Sarah will tell you that during all her early years she was fearful of even raising her hand in class and became very angry with us when we suggested she take a speech class to help overcome her apprehension of talking in front of people. At Landmark she

spoke on several panels; she has also spoken to groups of parents and educators and now gets less nervous than I do when speaking.

We are so grateful for what Sarah learned at Landmark, but are also extremely grateful to those who were her mentors and for the encouragement she received from them. Carolyn Olivier, John Bagge, and Diane Wood have always been in our minds as those who kept Sarah strong and focused with their support and encouragement.

When I think back to that visit to Landmark and recall such a gathering of people with similar challenges, people who can identify with one another and, perhaps for the first time in their lives, have found someone who understands them and what they have struggled with all their lives, I recall an article titled "Thy Name is Courage" that has stayed uppermost in my mind. This article by Trudy Winstead, an Academic Language Therapist, has had such an impact on me that I have read and re-read it many times. I try to share it with others who I want to be able to understand Sarah and what her life has been like all these years. This author understands how Sarah and I have struggled all these years and so, it truly breaks my heart to read it, but I know I have found someone who has voiced our suffering. I am most affected when I get to these couple of sentences:

When these students choose to *trust* again, they are vulnerable as never before. They risk everything. Therefore, if they summon the courage to honor us with their *trust*—if they indeed let us in—we must recognize and cherish this as their most sacred gift. And we must *never, never, never* let them down! *(emphasis mine)*[5]

After reading this article, I am often on my knees again, grateful because I know that only God could have given Sarah the strength and the courage to keep going. The article bids the questions: *Where did these students find this exceptional courage? Where does it come from? What replenishes it? Does it ever run out?* The answer, of course, in Sarah's life is, "only from God!" With the author's permission, I have included the article here.

"Thy Name Is Courage" by Trudy Winstead

Many of life's basic truths lie within the lyrics of today's country music. Listen to this: "In this world there's a whole lot of trouble, baby. In this world there's a whole lot of pain. In this world there's a whole lot of trouble, but a whole lot of ground to gain." Although Mary Chapin Carpenter wrote these lyrics, many of our students who learn differently certainly could have, for they know all about trouble, pain, and ground to gain. Every day, our students are bombarded with "how to gain ground" comments from well-intentioned teachers, parents, and friends. "You should do your homework." "You ought to spend more time on your assignments." "You need to see your teachers for help." "You must study harder." Should. Ought. Need. Must. These are words which our students know by heart—words they have come to dread. The "shoulds," "oughts," "needs," and "musts" are embedded in the phrases our students hear repeatedly, internalize over time, and eventually begin to believe about themselves. By middle or high school, many of them have been subjected to these admonitions so frequently that they have wrapped themselves tightly in a cloak of learned helplessness for protection from the pain they feel from never measuring up.

Learned Helplessness

Learned helplessness comes from years of effort with minimal reward. For our students, the amount of time and energy they invest rarely yields the desired result. Only infrequently do they experience a sense of mastery or pride in their work. They seldom feel successful and nothing they do seems to make any difference. Outside forces—parents, teachers, even scores and grades—rule their lives. And since they believe that events happen either to or around them, they feel powerless. In effect, our students find themselves trapped in a scene directed by others. Without choices or options, they become hopeless and helpless, settling into a pattern of academic passivity. Their locus of control gradually shifts from internal to external, and after a while they simply give up. By this time, they have also lost sight of their considerable strengths, because the voices that they hear most focus on what's wrong, not what's right. These voices also dwell on what should be fixed rather than what should be celebrated. The shoulds, oughts, needs, and musts constantly echo in their minds. Believing these echoes, our students feel guilt, shame, even despair. They become worn down. Drained. For them, continuing the fight is just too hard. And so they quit, allowing others to dictate, dominate, and judge. Then they stand by and witness their lives being run by others. And as they watch, they ache.

Disguises

Frequently our students find themselves intellectually and emotionally exhausted. They reach a point where they just want to tell the world they've had enough. Often, they send this message with actions rather than words. For instance, some students may bound into our classrooms marked as trouble-makers, class clowns, or chatterboxes. Others may slip in silently as conformists or pleasers. They may appear boisterous, lethargic, rambunctious, apathetic, obstreperous, timid, or daring. They also may be resistant, rebellious, angry, or hostile. In any case, they keep their emotional distance—disguised as someone they're not—for they dare not risk exposing their feelings of inadequacy or inferiority to anyone. And so, who they are is carefully hidden behind the protective masks that they wear.

Also concealed behind these masks is their constant and pervasive sensation of fear. Our students are always fearful that someone will uncover what they don't know. They dread being embarrassed in front of their friends and left open to ridicule by their enemies. They're frightened that they can't ever measure up to expectations—those of others as well as their own. Most of all, however, they're terrified that someone will discover their darkest secret—that they REALLY DO care and that they hurt. Therefore, many of our students who learn differently just give up because they can no longer muster the energy to keep going.

The Few...The Brave

However, there are a few who don't give up...a few who keep on fighting. Day after day. Week after week. Sometimes year after year. These are the same students who have also been beaten down by the system, enduring years of humiliation and blame. They, too, constantly stare failure in the face. Every day, they take a gigantic leap into the abyss of the unknown. Every waking moment, they gamble with their self-esteem. These students refuse to quit. They try. They stumble. They fall. They're down but not for long. Each time, they pick themselves up and start over, exhibiting a tenacity and a fortitude rarely seen in adults. Seemingly undaunted, they forge ahead, bravely risking exposure.

What sets them apart from all the rest? Where do they get their resilience and will power? What keeps them strong?

Courage

Courage. I think the answer is courage. Pure, raw courage. Nerve. Guts. Grit. A courage that most of us neither have nor understand. But sustaining this courage requires patience and mental toughness. In fact, being courageous is exhausting. Searching for and finding enough courage to continue for just one more day can leave even the strongest bone-tired and weary. And yet, drawing on seemingly limitless reserves from within, they go on. These are the gutsy. The valiant. The brave.

In addition to this courage, a small number demonstrate an even more remarkable kind of courage...the courage to trust. Us. Their parents, their teachers, their adult friends. Over time, most of these students have learned that sharing trust leaves them wide open to be disappointed, hurt, or betrayed. As a result, they trust no one and rely only on themselves—a lonely existence. So, if they ever decide to let us in to see what they know and what they don't—to see who they really are—they take a tremendous chance. They stand stripped and exposed before us, putting themselves in extreme emotional danger.

When these students choose to trust again,

they are vulnerable as never before. They risk everything. Therefore, if they summon the courage to honor us with their trust—if they indeed let us in—we must recognize and cherish this as their most sacred gift. And we must never, never, never let them down.

Their Gift to Me

Over the years, I have often wondered where these students found this exceptional courage. Where does it come from? What replenishes it? Does it ever run out? I don't know. I'll probably never understand. However, I do know one thing for certain. I know that what I learn from my students is far more valuable than what they learn from me. For these students teach about strength and endurance and heart. They show resilience, bravery, and determination. In countless ways, they let me in to witness their courage. Their lessons are life lessons...lessons that will remain cradled within me forever.

I stand in awe of these students. I marvel at their spirit. I view them with respect and admiration. They are my instructors, my role models, my mentors. They are, in fact, my heroes. Without question, they are the very reasons I keep trying. They are why I never give in. They are my energy and my strength. Witnessing their courage provides me with the motivation to constantly push myself to rise to new heights. They are, in fact, my heroes. They are the wind beneath my wings.

Many of life's basic truths lie within the lyrics of today's country music. Listen to what Jeff Silbar wrote: "Did you ever know that you are my hero? And everything I would like to be? I can fly higher than an eagle.... you are the wind beneath my wings."[6]

Chapter 20

"WHY, OH WHY, CAN'T YOU CLOSE THE CUPBOARD DOORS AND DRAWERS?"

"Come unto Me... and I will give you rest." Matthew 11:28

*S*hortly after reading the article "Thy Name is Courage," I found and read the book *Women with Attention Deficit Disorder* by Sari Solden. While reading that book, my mind began racing back to those earlier days at home. So this was the answer to so many of my frustrations! I thought back to all those days at home when I just couldn't understand and would question, *why, oh why, does she do the same things over and over again—won't she ever learn?* Those were the days before I really understood what attention deficit disorder (ADD) was—and before the medication prescribed by Dr. Abuzzahab. The answer was that Sarah had attention deficit disorder (ADD) all those years and I did not know it!

One of the most frustrating things that Sarah *always*

did when she was home was to leave the cupboard doors and drawers open or just slightly ajar. Actually, *any* door or drawer was left open. And then I read the book *Women with Attention Deficit Disorder*. In the book, the author responds to the question asked by so many, "Why do you leave everything open? Why don't you put things back?" Solden says that we, as parents or spouses, don't understand that the decision is not a conscious one. She conveys in her book that those with attention deficit disorder (ADD) truly are NOT aware of what they continue to do, or why, until someone points out to them that all the cupboard doors and drawers are open and things are just left lying around.[7] Reading this book is a "must" for understanding the core of what attention deficit disorder (ADD) is. Even though the title refers to women, this book is definitely for men and boys also.

So many other frustrations were addressed when I began reading other books. I would be so annoyed that Sarah would always leave her keys lying on the floor close to the door. "Sarah, pick up your keys and put them someplace else!" Her answer, one that I later accepted and truly did understand, was: "Mom, if I don't leave them there, I will never remember where I put them—now I always know they are by the front door." And another common complaint of mine: "Why do you always leave all your papers and bills lying all over the table? Put them in a file someplace." Her answer: "Out of sight, out of mind. If I don't *see* them, I will never remember to pay my bills." And to remember to take her medications, Sarah purchased a watch with a timer.

I would often be hurt if Sarah saw I was so busy and didn't offer to help me. After mentioning this to her one day she said, "All you have to do is ask me and I will be glad to help. It just *didn't enter my mind.*" Other times I found myself worrying when it got late at night and she still had not come home. One especially "trying" late night, she had fallen asleep on the sofa at a friend's home. "I would have called you, but it just *didn't enter my mind.* I didn't mean to worry you," she said.

One very annoying thing Sarah always did (and still does) was continually moving her foot while sitting. I would always say to her in church, "Stop moving your foot! It is very disturbing to others." And later, of course, I discovered this spontaneous movement was in the textbook information on attention deficit disorder (ADD). It was very helpful when Sarah and I could talk together about all of this without becoming emotionally involved, because she wanted desperately for me to understand her and I was yearning to identify and accept all of her actions relating to attention deficit disorder (ADD).

I also learned from my reading that "parental structure" can help in many areas of attention deficit disorder (ADD). I believe this did make a difference in one area of Sarah's life. Because of "disorganization" many individuals with attention deficit disorder (ADD) are constantly arriving late for events, appointments, meetings with friends, etc. In my family growing up my father was one of those who arrived *early* at meetings and such. His motto was: always be on time! Consequently, our family, and Sarah in particular, grew up always being on time wherever she went, whether it was to school, an appointment, with friends—because Mom made sure she left the house on time. Not knowing it at the time, this discipline has been a major benefit in Sarah's "grown-up" life! However, this parental structure did not seem to affect Sarah's disorganization and being messy! One day when Sarah was gone for the weekend, I decided to venture into her room and "organize" her piles! She came home and was very upset with me: "Mom, I knew where everything was in all of those piles and now you've mixed everything up!" She had a strategy that worked for her and now I had disrupted it.

I have read many books, subscribed to magazines on dyslexia and attention deficit disorder (ADD), became a member of IDA (International Dyslexic Association) and CHADD (Children and Adults with Attention Deficit Disorder) and attended several national conferences on dyslexia and attention deficit disorder (ADD). I was determined to avail myself of everything there was out there to understand Sarah and her disabilities. And it has made a huge difference in our relationship!

Rich (Dad), however, did not have the chance to read and attend the meetings and conferences that I had, so he tended to have a harder time understanding and accepting what Sarah was going through. I wrote the following in my journal one Saturday morning when Sarah was in high school:

Sarah has been under a lot of pressure with her classes and homework. She does work SO hard. Her father doesn't always realize that she really does work hard and puts in absolutely everything she has into her school work. But he has not been able to take advantage of all the books and conferences and outside input I have had to understand what a "disability" her learning disability really is. And he isn't always around to see how hard she works. She does put so much energy into her learning and, therefore, she also needs some release from this pressure. So, many times exercising or TV is okay—just in order to unwind and relax. But again, her Dad does not always understand this.

This morning was an example of this—but it is also an example of Sarah's growing in her spiritual life. Maybe I should say it is an example of God's working in Sarah's life! She was taking a break and exercising on the small exercise trampoline we have set up in the family room, when her Dad saw it, and assumed she was just wasting time. He told her she should be studying instead and in all kinds of words indicated to her (without realizing it) that she certainly does not put into her school work what she should. (You know, all those good things parents have a way of saying when we are upset!) And, of course, she knew in fact how much she had been putting into school. I knew she was really hurt. I don't remember what she said, but she left the tramp and went upstairs to her bedroom and slammed the door! This broke my heart, as she needs so much our support and encouragement, and definitely not to tear her down. After talking with Rich, he was truly sorry about his attitude and really had not meant to make her feel bad.

According to past experience, Sarah would stay in her room for awhile and the rest of the day would be really moody, with a bad attitude and all that goes along with that. Well—the exciting thing—in about 10-15 minutes she came back downstairs and got back on the tramp. I can't remember exactly what she said, but everything seemed to be alright from then on. She began talking with her Dad as if nothing had happened! I believe God touched her heart that day! Thank you, God!

Since those early years Rich and I have both grown in our understanding of dyslexia and attention deficit disorder (ADD). Rich began attending meetings with me, and I tried to share with him any new information I would get to help him comprehend all the manifestations of dyslexia and attention deficit disorder (ADD). Sarah stayed close to her Dad and was always eager to have him involved in her activities. The medication for attention deficit disorder (ADD) has made a huge difference in Sarah's life. We all began to live a less stressful life when we learned to observe and ask questions before we would judge any actions. Thank you, thank you, God!

Chapter 21

"TEN TURBULENT YEARS"

"Your road led by a pathway through the sea...a pathway no one knew was there!" Psalms 77:19

*S*arah completed the fall semester of 1991 at Landmark College. We were so grateful for what this experience meant to Sarah and her future! She had been at Landmark for the five-week summer program and the next full year; now after this fall semester it was decided she would return to Minneapolis.

Sarah was returning to Minneapolis...but to what? After Sarah came home from Landmark, the next ten years of her life seemed to be years without a goal or even a real purpose. My mind continually focused on the plaque in our bookcase:

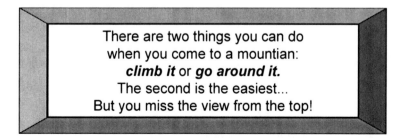

There are two things you can do
when you come to a mountian:
climb it or ***go around it.***
The second is the easiest...
But you miss the view from the top!

These words reminded me of Sarah's determination and convinced me that she wanted to make it to the top. But now, in these years of her life, it seemed that, while she was not struggling, she was also no longer "climbing" on her way to the "top." It was as if she was stranded just short of the top of the mountain. She was productive during those years, but was she reaching for her potential? And then one morning I listened to a powerful song by Ray Boltz titled "Give Me Your Hand"[8]:

> I was climbing up a mountain, headed for the top
> My feet started sliding and I almost fell off
> I landed on a rocky ledge, suspended in the air
> And I cried out in despair
> I said, "Is anybody out there? Anybody there at all?"
> Then I saw Him reaching down and I heard Him call:
>
> CHORUS:
> Give me your hand, I'll lift you up
> Don't be afraid, you just have to trust
> I have been there in the place you stand
> There's no need to fear, that's why I'm here
> Give me your hand

After listening to this song that morning, I fell to my knees once again— *Yes, Lord, you are there. There is no need to fear, we just have to trust!*

Those ten years were turbulent, but they were anything

but "uneventful!" In my mind, those years were filled with much turbulence and uncertainty; they were years that proved to demand even more faith and trust on my part. My broken heart for Sarah's future drew me to my knees more fervently as I lived with her through years of uncertainty. I wrote this in my journal one day during those turbulent years:

At this time in my life when I think about Sarah's life from maybe third grade on...I am almost smothered and emotionally overwhelmed by the circumstances in her life and what she has had to overcome. I am overwhelmed by what this "child" has had to endure...what each day of her young life through adulthood held for her...what she had to wake up to each day! This was everything from dyslexia and attention deficit disorder (ADD), which meant struggling daily in school all the way through college...to living with dyslexia and attention deficit disorder (ADD) in the work world...to numerous physical issues after graduating from high school...to injury and complications from a pedestrian auto accident...to financial issues after being betrayed by two friends. And each day knowing she would have to endure and be strong for "just one more day." This is absolutely emotionally overwhelming to me.

But…the most overwhelming and powerful emotion is recognizing **the presence of God in each of those days**…in her days and in mine! Looking back I am again most overwhelmed by the knowledge that truly: **"THE BATTLE BELONGS TO THE LORD!"**

Each day of those ten turbulent years God kept me in His peace; He reminded me daily of His faithfulness and the need to continue to TRUST Him!

Chapter 22

"THIS IS JERRY AT THE PARK HOUSE."

"Oh, give thanks to the Lord, for His lovingkindness continues forever." Psalms 136:1

Several times during those turbulent ten years, my mind would return to an incident when Sarah was in grade school. This powerful touch in Sarah's life always encouraged me again and again that God was holding Sarah in the palm of His hand.

I answered the phone one afternoon to an alarming message from Jerry at the neighborhood park. I practically fell to my knees as Jerry was telling me what had just happened to Sarah.

Sarah and her friends were playing foosball in the recreation center at the neighborhood park, as they often did after school. However...as she was playing she also had a candy jawbreaker in her mouth! We all had heard over and over again and tried to tell our kids, "Be very careful about jawbreakers...you could swallow it and choke on it!"

Now Sarah had done exactly that—she had swallowed the jawbreaker and was choking! Her friends ran in a panic to find Jerry; as he was approaching her he could see that she was already weaving and foaming at the mouth! Jerry was trained in the Heimlich maneuver and quickly grabbed her from behind. As he performed the maneuver, the jawbreaker did, in fact, pop right out of her mouth!

He said she was doing just fine, but thought it would be best if I would come to the park to walk home with her. She was very, very shaken and spent the rest of the evening pretty quiet and did not want to talk about it. I was very shaken as well, and spent part of my evening on my knees in thanksgiving to God for His overwhelming mercy and care for Sarah!

Thank you...thank you...thank you, God!

Chapter 23

"MRS. HOLTE, SARAH WAS HIT BY A CAR!"

"I will both lay me down in peace, and sleep; for thou, LORD, only makes me dwell in safety." Psalms 4:8

*A*nd then there was another call that I remember so well—even where I was sitting and what time it was! Sarah's friend, Mark, was calling from San Francisco. I was at work sitting at my desk when the call came.

Mark was from San Francisco and had been in Minneapolis on business. About ten days earlier he had driven back to San Francisco. He knew how much Sarah loved being with her friends in San Francisco, so he had asked her if she would like to ride back with him, help with driving, and then spend time with friends before flying back to Minneapolis. Of course she jumped at the idea! At the time she was working in Minneapolis again as a waitress and her schedule could be very flexible.

When I got the call from Mark, Sarah had only been in San Francisco a few days. He began to fill me in on Sarah's status: she had been hit by a car, she had a minor head injury, and she was in the emergency room at San Francisco General Hospital, but she was going to be just fine. Mark told me that Sarah would be calling me in just a little while when she got out of the emergency room. The entire time he was talking, all I really heard was that she had been hit by a car, and she was going to be okay. Of course, to me, the words "hit by a car" meant that she had been driving Mark's car when another car hit her.

I hung up the phone, told my co-workers what had happened, and waited for Sarah's call. When Sarah called several hours later she told me "the rest of the story." Had I actually listened and heard the whole story when Mark was telling me, I know I would have panicked. The real incident was that Sarah, *as a pedestrian*, was crossing the street in the retail section of San Francisco when a van hit her and knocked her down. She truly had been "hit by a car!" She was unconscious when the ambulance came and took her to San Francisco General Hospital. She did have a head injury but was told it was not critical. They were able to treat it with stitches and sent her home. She called me as soon as she reached her friend's house and said she would be flying home tomorrow as soon as she could get a flight. I was not terribly panicked as long as she sounded good and said she would be home the next day.

Rich and I picked Sarah up the next day and were so relieved to see that she was, in fact, okay. She stayed at our home to recover from the impact of the accident. Besides her head injury, her body was bruised as well. These were the injuries we could see at the time. The full impact of the accident on her life would not be evident until later. Sarah's only memory of the accident was her ride in the ambulance. She tells how the paramedics believed she was doing just fine because she was "jabbering" to them during the whole ride. Her first thoughts when she became conscious in the ambulance were of scenes from the TV series *ER*. She knew she had to stay awake, because in *ER*, it was the patient who lost consciousness that died on the way to the hospital. She "jabbered" and talked to the paramedics all the way to the hospital in order to stay awake...and stay alive!

As time went on Sarah suffered many physical and emotional consequences of the accident, even though the trauma did not become evident until about a month later. It became obvious that she would need medical care for an extended period of time. Because the accident was in California, we were in touch with an attorney there to work with the insurance company of the driver of the van. One year later, the case ended up in a trial. Below is our statement to the insurance company and attorney about our perspective of the effects of the accident on Sarah's life.

"OUR" SARAH...
Perspectives from Mom and Dad

- Overwhelming concern because of head injury and unknown long-term effects and impact on future

- Change in personality from carefree and independent to very anxious and inward because of dizziness and unsteady balance
- Concern over her day-to-day activities; always a little on edge not knowing when she may become dizzy and lose her balance...on a number of occasions we have been called to pick her up from an event because of becoming dizzy and nauseated
- Restless nights of sleep because of waking up dizzy and with vertigo
- HUGE impact on her future...having learned how to manage her learning disabilities, she was ready to move forward with solid plans toward her life goals and now these would be put on hold
- Shortness of breath is constant
- Chest pains and needs medication
- Severe pain in neck and shoulders
- Some short-term memory loss
- Accident has virtually taken two years out of her life
- Unsteady and interrupted work life because of many, many doctor's appointments
- Much therapy
- Trips back and forth to California for meetings with attorney

- Leaving work because of dizziness and nausea
- Volumes of paperwork for insurance, doctors, and attorneys
- Unable to pursue her school interests and job search because of above reasons
- Accident has taken an enormous toll on her emotional life
- Concern for health
- Concern for future in the market place
- Concern for financial security, which is overwhelming in light of medical bills thus far
- Anxiety is ever-present (and seems to have affected personality, because she never seemed to be anxious or experience tension)
- Having trouble handling normal, everyday stress
- Cannot be in large groups of people

We felt her disappointment when she realized she will have to give up her dream of living in a city, such as San Francisco or New York, because of the dizzy sensation of just being on city streets with crowds of people surrounding her and approaching from all directions. She will not be able to ride a bicycle or ski. She cannot ride an escalator or walk along a second-floor railing at the mall.

No words can express the overwhelming emotions felt when a loved one is hurting and struggling and the future of this bright, talented, loving, and vivacious child is in question. However, we as her parents know and hold on to several things:

- she IS a survivor
- she has an incredible attitude and personality
- she has a very strong faith
- she has a strong family for support
- she is deeply loved
- God is in control of her life!

We also sent the following note to Sarah's friends and supporters:

Dear Friend,

Would you be willing to remember Sarah in your prayers on August 9th? She will be with two lawyers for most of the day giving a deposition on her pedestrian accident two years ago. She especially needs God's peace and strength…and also needs a clear mind and a calm spirit. Please pray that she will feel God's presence in a very close and personal way and will be able to leave everything in His hands.

Please also pray for the driver of the van who hit her, as he will be giving his deposition the next day...his name is Jerod. (Pray for his mother as well!)

<u>Additional note</u>: Just thought I would tell you a little of what is going on in Sarah's life right now. On June 6, 1998, she was hit by a van while crossing the street in San Francisco. She had a head injury for which she has been seeing doctors ever since. After two years they have now determined that this is a permanent injury to the central nervous system. Her symptoms are dizziness and balance problems. She gets dizzy every night while sleeping, is not able to be in large crowds, never knows when the dizziness may hit her, can't run, bike, or do any of the physical things she used to do, and in general is less focused and has lost some of her spirit. Her medical bills are mounting, and that is a real concern to her. Consequently, she is very stressed and is now also experiencing many stress-related symptoms.

The two insurance companies are now trying to settle this and, of course, Sarah is in the middle. The other insurance company is attempting to blame her dizziness and loss of balance on her dyslexia. She is strong, has a solid faith, and is a "survivor," but she is really struggling right now.

Thank you for your support! God is faithful, and Sarah is in His hands!

This accident certainly put Sarah's life "on hold." She endured a very short one-day trial in California where she was asked to give her deposition. Ultimately, she was awarded a monetary settlement to cover her medical expenses. Sarah realized that, because of the accident, there was no way she could leave Minneapolis now. Instead of dealing with learning issues, she was now struggling with the impact of the accident on her life, both physically and emotionally.

After recovering from the immediate physical issues of the accident, she began working for a wonderful caterer doing private catering. (And was I ever thankful, because Sarah was learning to be a creative cook…and cooking was something she was not going to learn from me!) The food presentation she learned was amazing! Her schedule could now be fairly flexible; this was a blessing because of all the accident-related issues facing her, including many doctor appointments. Along with her catering position, she began working again as a waitress.

It was during this time that Sarah would call me to pick her up from work because she was dizzy or experiencing vertigo. She struggled with these physical issues for at least two years after the accident. There were also emotional after-effects. Because of her struggles, Sarah lived at home during these years, and it was especially painful to watch her personality change. She had never been anxious or tense around people, but after the accident she seemed to want to stay close to home when she was not working. She became less focused and increasingly uninterested in the world around her. As her parents, it was so hard to see this vibrant, outgoing, full-of-life daughter lose so much of her spirit and become so tense. Many visits to the neurologist eventually led to a diagnosis of a permanent injury to the central nervous system. Sarah's future certainly looked much different than either she or we had planned or hoped for. However, the future *we* had envisioned for Sarah's life was *not* the future *God* had planned for her.

As each of the next two years passed, Sarah's overwhelming symptoms began to disappear. What the doctors had predicted for her future was not to be. Sarah still feels the effects of the neck injury from time to time. However, to this day she does not experience any of the symptoms of the accident that we had so dreaded! God had His own plans for her life...and for this powerful answer to prayer, my usual cry of *Thank you, God!* seemed oh so feeble! There is no way to thank God enough. Instead, we only pray that our lives can be a witness to our gratitude!

Chapter 24

"MOM, LET'S FIND HIM AND BUY HIM A NEW BACKPACK!"

"It is more blessed to give than to receive." Acts 20:35

Sarah has always had a "big" heart! As I related at the beginning of this book, I recognized her generous spirit early when she was in a relay and held out her hand for her friend to catch up. Sarah always wanted to help someone on a street corner. When she was a freshman at Westmont, we sent her money for her birthday. She didn't have much money during college, and we thought she may want to buy something for herself. But what did she do instead? She took a friend to dinner because she said he needed a good meal. When she was a junior, her birthday money went to buy a friend a sweatshirt because "he needed it."

One day, when Sarah and I were shopping at the mall, we decided to separate and meet in an hour. She actually came looking for me before the hour was up. She told me she saw an older man who she felt was obviously homeless just wandering the mall. He had a very ragged backpack with an oxygen tank.

Could we quickly go find him and buy him a new backpack? We did walk the mall to try to find him, but we never did. She was very disappointed! She truly is very compassionate. To this day you will find her opening her window to hand some cash to someone on the corner...or a used coat to someone in need. Unfortunately, twice during those ten turbulent years her "big" heart was taken advantage of...in a big way!

After Sarah's car accident, the insurance company awarded her a small monetary settlement intended to cover her future medical bills. As Rich and I were in the process of researching a secure and wise place to invest the money from this settlement, a "friend" who was in the financial business convinced Sarah to allow him to invest it for her. He promised a substantial return on her money in a very short time. She told us about the transaction *after* she had given him the money. It seemed a little "too good to be true," but it was too late to interfere. About six months later she, too, learned it *was* too good to be true.

Several years later, while Sarah was working and earning money, her "big" heart was again taken advantage of. She loaned a sizable amount of money to a "friend" and was never paid back. She suffered financially for years because of this betrayal!

Both of these betrayals once again tested what I believe about my loving God. And God held Sarah and me even more tightly in the palm of His hand through this devastating time of heartbreak, betrayal, and panic. I was continually reminded of some of my daily devotions over the years:

"Perfect trust in God—such a trust that we no longer want God's blessings, but only want God Himself. Have we come to the point where God can withdraw His blessings from us without our trust in Him being affected?"[9] *Oswald Chambers*

"Can you thank Me for trusting you with this experience even if I never tell you why?" *Helen Roseveare*

"God does not give us overcoming life—He gives us life as we overcome."[10] *Oswald Chambers*

"Never look for justice in this world, but never cease to give it."[11] *Oswald Chambers*

I continued to pray for Sarah and these two friends, as well, and once again turned everything over into God's hands. Sarah was never bitter, but she was so badly hurt by these betrayals. She certainly learned about praying for God's wisdom in all things.

We both forgave these friends, left them in God's hands, and trusted God with Sarah's future.

Chapter 25

"MOM, CAN YOU COME QUICKLY?"

"May God bless you richly and grant you increasing freedom from all anxiety and fear!" I Peter 1:2

While Sarah was living in Minneapolis, we received a panicked phone call in the middle of the morning. Could we come quickly to her apartment? She was in excruciating pain and her roommate was not at home. As Rich and I jumped into the car, I was now also panicking. She lived about twenty minutes from our home, and I knew that she more than likely needed to get to a hospital quickly. I called her from the car as we were driving and found out that her roommate had come home and they were now on their way to the hospital.

We changed course and were now headed to the hospital. When we arrived, I found her on a bed in the emergency room. She was in unbearable pain! The doctor had just come in with the diagnosis: she had a kidney stone. Before he performed any more procedures, the doctor ordered morphine to counter the pain. I was in the room as she received a shot of morphine. It could not have been more than ninety seconds from the moment she was writing in pain until the morphine took effect. It was pretty amazing to witness the immediate effect of the medication—from overwhelming pain to absolute calm in about ninety seconds!

After several weeks of hoping the stone would move by itself, Sarah had surgery to remove the kidney stone. I was so grateful that Sarah was in Minneapolis during this emergency and subsequent surgery. She missed only a week of work and then was back on schedule.

Then Sarah began to be concerned about her right arm. I was certain this numbness in her right arm was due to all the writing she had done with this hand after enrolling in Landmark. However, the numbness was persistent, and it interfered with many activities. Then I remembered some-thing that worried me: numbness can be a sign of multiple sclerosis (MS), and a member of my extended family had died from MS. However, after much testing and several times of the painful pin-prick test, the doctor determined it was a radial nerve problem in her right arm and she would need surgery.

Sarah had surgery while she was in Minneapolis, but continued to have pain in that arm. Even though several trips to the Mayo Clinic after surgery confirmed that the surgery was successful, Sarah still spent several more years with pain in that arm and hand.

Through all of this, Sarah remained strong and determined to live her life without complaining or feeling sorry for herself. She remained grateful for the life God had given her.

My marked-up Bible is a witness to the many times I sat in a waiting room while God spoke to me through His Word. God continually gave me His peace and reminded me of His many promises. One promise I always did cling to: *She is My child...I will not forget her...I have carved her on the palm of my hand.*

Chapter 26

"CALM DOWN, LADY...YOU WILL NOT HAVE TO PAY THIS PHONE BILL!"

"I will praise the Lord no matter what happens."

Psalms 34:1

ventually, Sarah was hired by a local restaurant, part of a nationwide chain, as a server, trainer, and office manager. She stayed in Minneapolis until 1998, when a job opened up at the chain's headquarters in Colorado. She accepted the position, moving to Colorado to work as administrative assistant to the Vice President of Operations.

One more time, Rich and I found ourselves waving "goodbye" as we watched her drive off in her little white "Beetle," following the van carrying everything she owned. She was moving in with a friend in Louisville, Colorado. Before Sarah left, to make *Mom* feel better, we bought cell phones for both Sarah and me and put them both on one cell phone plan.

About a month after she had her cell phone, I opened the first bill. How does one describe the kind of anger that I felt? I was absolutely filled with rage! *What* was Sarah thinking? Did she call *everyone* she knew...and talk for hour upon hour? The cell phone bill was $1,136! I was panicked, confused, and very angry with her. I was shaking as I immediately called her. She was quick to assure me that those were not her charges on the phone bill. Could I believe her? I was still shaking, as I next called the cell phone company. I quickly heard, "*Calm down, lady...calm down!* You won't have to pay this bill! *Calm down!*"

After taking one look at the bill, the phone company promptly determined what had happened. They assured me that Sarah, in fact, had *not* made all those calls! All but a few of the calls had been made by drug dealers in Miami! But... but...! Again I heard, "Calm down...no, you will *not* have to pay this bill!"

How had this happened? The phone company explained to me that at one point, when Sarah was driving through an underpass while traveling across the country, someone was above with a device to collect her cell phone number. And that someone subsequently used her number for many drug deals! I took another more detailed look at the bill and immediately saw the many, many, many calls from the Miami area. I, of course, was overwhelmed with relief! No...we did *not* have to pay this $1,136 cell phone bill!

Thank you...thank you...thank you, God!

Our cell phone numbers were changed and we continued to stay connected by phone while Sarah lived in Colorado.

Sarah loved the daily drive through the mountains to Denver. She loved being with friends. However, from time to time she would share with me about her job. It didn't take long before I heard what she was really experiencing at work. As an administrative assistant she was responsible for, among other things, a lot of correspondence. One day she shared with me, "Mom, there is no way I should stay in this job. I really can't write a good letter for the manager." Once again, Sarah was experiencing the effect of her learning disabilities. While Landmark College had helped immensely with her writing skills, they were not at the skill level required of an administrative assistant. She was terribly embarrassed to tell her boss about her inability to perform her job as expected. However, she eventually did share this with him. Even though he was very compassionate about her situation, they both agreed that leaving this position would be the right decision. So, in September of 1998, Sarah picked up and moved all her things back to Minneapolis. Later Sarah shared with me what one of her co-workers in Colorado wrote upon her leaving.

Sarah was sad to leave, but again knew that it was the best decision

FUN SARAH

Obviously it will be less exciting without "FUN" Sarah...

...colors will be muted
...sounds less intense
...conversations less energizing
...visits will be imperative!

for her at the time. Although she returned to Minneapolis to her many friends and she knew she could easily find a job, Sarah was still restless and searching. Since California was always her dream location, it wasn't long until she moved to San Francisco to work and live with a high school friend. But, again, as much as she loved California, this move still did not seem to be the answer to what she was searching for in her life. She stayed in San Francisco less than a year and then moved back to Minneapolis...again!

Chapter 27

"AND WHAT WAS MOM DOING ALL THOSE YEARS?"

"But those who wait on the Lord shall renew their strength." Isaiah 40:31

While Sarah's years at Westmont and Landmark were stressful, they were also a time when she was on a path of growth and discovery…making that difficult but rewarding "climb to the top." But the years *after* Landmark seemed so directionless. Sarah seemed more like she was wandering in a wilderness than climbing a mountain.

God had blessed Sarah with a positive outlook and upbeat spirit, but deep down I knew she was struggling. Through those years I would leave little notes of encouragement or share with her my heartfelt feelings, such as the following:

Sarah…

This is truly a "wilderness experience" for you right now…and who wants a "wilderness experience"! But…only in the wilderness is

174

God the very closest He can be to us! He does not allow "wilderness experiences" for everyone, but when He does, He has something special in mind. When He does allow it, He plans to be there in it as well. He will plan to be there in such a personal and close way with a love so very deep for you! You will get to know Him in a very personal way...your Heavenly Father!

In looking back one can hardly believe that God would choose "me" to be that close to...and I will never be the same! It is as if I am the only child He has in the whole world. Sarah, you know how much I love you and how desperately I want you to be happy and find in life what is the best for you. Well...I was thinking the other evening...**Can you even imagine that God loves you much, much more than I do**! I can hardly believe that, because I love you so much...but it is absolutely *true*! I would do anything for you...but God *can* do anything for you...He has the power to do anything and everything. And He loves you so much and wants the very, very best for you. And not only that... He *knows* what is the very, very best for you.

Because He loves you even more than I do...just imagine how much He feels for you when you hurt and are sad and struggling and things do not go right! He loves much more than a Mother can...and that is so hard to believe...but *I believe it*!

Sarah...I know it is very, very hard to be thankful now, but the very, very best thing you can do right now is to find little things in each day to thank God for. We stay close to Him by noticing all the "little" things each day that He is in. Praise Him for who He is in your life...and what He is going to do in your life! It is sometimes helpful to write things on a piece of paper each day..."little" things in which we can see God working, "little" things for which we are grateful..."little" things that we noticed.

Stay so very close to Him by reading His Word and talking to Him...so that you can "know" how He wants you to go. GOD IS SO FAITHFUL! He never goes back on His promises...and He has PROMISED "to show you the way."

I love you SO much! Just know that God allows me to be close to you when I pray... and that I kneel by your bed every morning and night and talk with God about you and put you in His hands. **I put my trust in Him because I know the things He has done in**

my life...and in your life...and He will do it again!

KEEP YOUR EYES UPON JESUS!

We love you!

And this note:

Sarah...

I wonder if you really remember how much God has touched your life...how much He loves you...how much He wants the **very, very best** for your life...how many times He has been there and you may not have even realized...how your life is 100% in His hands...and He has complete control of everything that happens in your life (unless you tell Him you don't want that anymore)... and He has the **POWER** to control your life. Do you know that the **POWER** He has in your life is that same **POWER** that raised Jesus from the dead! **WOW!**

Sarah, when you were struggling so in school (and in life in general) because of dyslexia and ADD, most mornings after you left for school (and Dad had left for work), I would sit down at the piano. I sang a number of songs (at the top of my voice, many times with tears streaming down my face) **praising God** and praying for Him to give you His peace.

I believe He did give you peace, Sarah... but He also gave me tremendous peace as well! I love you!

Many of my notes were just short words of encouragement. During those turbulent years Sarah was living with friends, so I would just leave the notes on her bed or dresser when I visited her apartment. She rarely acknowledged them, but I am convinced God used them to speak to her.

As I related earlier, those years demanded even more *faith* and *trust* than ever before! So, what was Mom doing all this time? I was on my knees, relying on and trusting God with the child I had placed in His hands so many years before!

> *For this child I prayed; and the Lord has granted me my petition which I made to Him. Therefore I have lent [her] to the Lord. As long as [she] lives, [she] is lent to the Lord.* 1 Samuel 1:27–28

Praise music became such an important part of my life during those years. At one point during Sarah's high school years, while I was experiencing my own trauma, I felt a special touch from God, which connected me so powerfully with Him through music. It was important to never forget that time in my life, so this too was recorded in my journal. I later shared the following entry with Sarah:

GOD'S OVERWHELMING AND
UNEXPLAINABLE PEACE!
"Thou wilt keep him in perfect peace whose mind is stayed on Him." Isaiah 26:3 (KJV)

I cannot share adequately the peace that comes to me when I am able to totally trust the Lord with my life. I am the one who goes to the doctor for a physical exam and then becomes paranoid about answering the telephone for fear some test did not turn out all right. What I have tried to share with my family and friends has been that if God can take a person like me and give me His perfect peace when I totally trust Him, He can do it for them also.

My life will never be perfectly anxiety free, but after an experience a number of years ago, my life has been changed. The doctor *did* call after my annual physical to tell me that I needed a breast biopsy because he didn't like what he saw on my routine mammogram. About a year before, a friend had

179

died of breast cancer, and cancer seemed to be all around me, so my immediate reaction was panic. I made an appointment immediately to see the surgeon that afternoon, but stopped long enough to see a friend, who has been a real prayer partner. She prayed with me and reminded me that God had already gone before me in this situation and was with me even now. I read a devotional book of mine in the waiting room about turning all these fears over to God and refusing these thoughts; by the time the doctor arrived to discuss the surgery I couldn't believe myself. I knew that God had prepared me for this day...I could sit there and actually talk about cancer with unbelievable peace. The entire week before the surgery was unexplainable. I shared with a friend that I was crying not because I was frightened, but because I was so grateful for the peace God had brought me. I had determined I would have no other thoughts but God on my mind. I began singing praise songs with my earphones and Walkman all day long. I learned to live one day at a time (even one hour at a time) and leave the rest in God's hands. And this certainly wasn't the "old" me, because my mind was used to racing ahead and coming to all sorts of conclusions.

The night before surgery was absolutely unreal; there is no other way to explain it. Normally, with even the smallest crisis, my mind would be going a mile a minute, there was a terrible feeling in the pit of my stomach, and I would have a foreboding feeling all during the night and upon awakening in the morning. That night I knew there were many friends praying for me, but I had no idea of the power of those prayers until that evening...I was singing praise songs before I went to bed; I laid down to go to sleep and I absolutely couldn't even get my mind to *think* about tomorrow! ABSOLUTELY MIRACULOUS! If that isn't the peace that Paul is talking about in Philippians! *"And God's peace, which is far more wonderful than the human mind can understand... His peace will keep your thoughts and your hearts quiet and at rest as you trust in Christ Jesus."* (Philippians 4:7).

I'm confident I would have been able to accept the word "cancer" if that had been the report, but for this time in my life God allowed the report to be "benign." And from that week on, I knew I would have many days of questioning, and all my anxiety would not be erased forever...but because of the experience of that week, I knew I never again would doubt God's presence in my life and that, no matter what happened in my life, He would be there for me! His Word taught me to **trust** Him, leave all in His hands, be patient during **His silences**, and wait for **His timing**. This truly brings me overwhelming and unexplainable **peace**!

Along with prayer, my quiet time with God, and music, I was also supported and encouraged by the faith of my two very close friends. These two special friends were always there to pray with me, share with me…and have breakfast or lunch together! Without the support of these friends, those ten "turbulent" years would have been lonely and much more stressful.

I used my Walkman nearly every day to sing praise songs more and more! I think the following two songs from the Maranatha Singers began my musical journey of peace and trust: "Lord, You're Worthy" and "I Want to Praise You, Lord!" Both of these songs reminded me to keep my focus on the Lord, to praise and worship Him despite difficult cir-cumstances, and—most of all—to believe in Him and trust Him. Every day I would lift Sarah up to the Lord and leave her in His hands, being reminded over and over again—by another song by the Maranatha Singers—that God would fulfill His purpose "In His Time!"

Several songs by Ray Boltz were especially powerful

during this time, especially "Another Child to Hold" and "Always Be a Child." The song "Another Child to Hold" was probably the most powerful song for me in those days. The lyrics to this song, written and sung by Ray Boltz, are as follows[13]:

> She looks down at her angel
> Sleeping in his bed
> She gently kneels beside him
> And then she bows her head
> And just like other mothers
> Who lived so long ago
> She brings her child to Jesus
> And gives him to the Lord
>
> CHORUS:
> Jesus, here's another child to hold
> Keep this child safe and warm
> This world can be so cold
> Take this child in Your arms
> And never let him go
> Jesus, here's another child to hold
>
> He watched his only daughter
> Leaving on a date
> He doesn't want to worry
> But now it's getting late
> Waiting in the darkness

He kneels down on the floor
And offers up a silent prayer
As he listens for the door

Wherever there are children, Lord
In danger or in need
May you find someone there
Praying on their knees
Oh, please…
Jesus, here's another child to hold
Jesus, here's my precious child
Jesus, here's another child

Oh, how I identified with this mother and father! I sang this song over and over and over again, knowing that Sarah truly was out in the "cold" world. And it gave me so much comfort and peace to know that God truly was holding her in His arms—He would keep her safe and warm and would never let her go.

The song "Always Be a Child" reminded me that God was there when Sarah (and each of us as well) took her first breath, that He was very near and heard her when she cried. This song was a reminder that she (and we) would always be His child even as we grow old. Another important piece of this song is that God was there the first time that we prayed. It reminds us how many promises we make and how often we fail, but each time we acknowledge we have sinned, God will always pick us up and hold us close again. If you can find a copy of Ray

Boltz's album titled *Another Child to Hold*, you should listen to both of these songs—the words are so powerful when you hear Ray Boltz sing them.

The lyrics in another song by Ray Boltz hit me one day like a bolt of lightning. His song, "Shepherd Boy," is based on I Samuel 16:10-12 and is about David being chosen as the next king of Israel, even though he was just a "shepherd boy" in the field. The song reminds us that when the king of Israel was being chosen, all of Jesse's sons, except David the youngest, stood before Samuel the prophet to be considered for king. No one thought to call David from the field, because surely the youngest would not ever wear the crown of a king—he was just a shepherd boy. But even though everyone else saw just a shepherd boy, God saw a king—and David, the shepherd boy, *was* chosen to be the king of Israel! *Yes,* I thought as I listened to this song, *God may see something altogether different for Sarah than I see...than the world sees!* So I wrote my own version of Ray Boltz's song to remind myself how God may see Sarah (however, none of it rhymes!):

> Well, she wasn't the neatest; she wasn't the boldest
> Chosen by our God
> Yet they called her brave and filled with courage
> They loved her all the more
> When others see a struggling kid, God may see a champ!
> **When others see an aimless girl, God may see a princess!**

When others ask, Who is she? God exclaims, She is
Mine!

We have a plaque in our home for each of our children
with the meaning of their given names. The meaning of the
name *Sarah* is "God's Princess." Ever since she was a child
and I found her name plaque, I was constantly finding little
things with a "Princess" theme and bringing them home for
her...even though I have a feeling she got pretty tired of it.
So, "Princess" just seemed the right attribute for this song.

There is another song that has also been very special to
me. I can still feel the emotions that I felt as I was sitting in
church with a friend of mine when the choir began singing
"On Eagle's Wings," by Jan Michael Joncas. It was during
an especially trying time for Sarah and this powerful song—
based on Psalms 91 and Isaiah 40:31—hit me and assured
me once again that Sarah was in the palm of His hands and
that He will raise her up above the terror and confusion.
Neither Sarah nor I need fear, because He is faithful. He is
her Rock and Refuge...and in *this* we trust! The following
are the Scriptures on which this beautiful song is based:

Psalms 91:1-2, 5, 11-12 (NKJV)

*He who dwells in the secret place of the
Most High shall abide under the shadow of
the Almighty.*

*I will say of the LORD, "He is my refuge and
my fortress; my God, in Him I will trust"...*

You shall not be afraid of the terror by night, nor of the arrow that flies by day...

For He shall give His angels charge over you, to keep you in all your ways. In their hands they shall bear you up, lest you dash your foot against a stone.

Isaiah 40:31 (NKJV)

But those who wait on the LORD Shall renew their strength; they shall mount up with wings like eagles, they shall run and not be weary, they shall walk and not faint.

Yet another song from the Maranatha Singers calmed me each morning: "In the Quiet of the Morning," which was about worshiping God in the early morning hours. I was working outside the home during most of those ten turbulent years, so my devotional quiet time was during the early morning hours and in the evening before bed. However, many years before, after taking to heart the book *Practicing the Presence* by Brother Lawrence, I was powerfully aware of being in God's presence each moment of every day. And that meant that I could talk with Him all through the day...and I did!

I have many versions of the Bible, but my personal Bible, which I have used since very early in Sarah's life, is *The Living Bible*. While I use another version of the Bible for study, *The Living Bible* is my devotional guide.

My Bible, along with two other books, *My Utmost for His Highest* by Oswald Chambers and *Come Away My Beloved* by Frances J. Roberts, are my constant companions; all three are ragged, marked up, and tattered from use.

One day Sarah was looking at my Oswald Chambers book. She looked up at me and said, "Mom, don't you want a new one?" Without hesitation, I said, "No way!" So it was, each day I was reminded by these three "old friends," my well-worn devotional books, that God was beside me and would never, ever leave me nor forsake me...or Sarah!

During one of my daily devotions, a passage from *My Utmost for His Highest* spoke to me in the depths of my heart. Because this devotional has been such a strong voice in my spiritual life all these years, I have no doubt that I had read this passage before, but now it spoke to me "for just such a time as this." The devotional, from October 11th, was titled "God's Silence—Then What?"

Because to this day, this message has so much meaning to me, I want to share it in its entirety here (with permission from the publisher):

"God's Silence—Then What?"

"When He heard that [Lazarus] was sick
He stayed two more days in the place
where He was." John 11:6

Has God trusted you with His *silence*—a *silence* that has great meaning? God's *silences* are actually His answers. Just think of those days of absolute *silence* in the home at Bethany! Is there anything comparable to those days in your life? Can God trust you like that, or are you still asking Him for a visible answer? God will give you the very blessings you ask if you refuse to go any further without them, but His *silence* is the sign that He is bringing you into an even more wonderful understanding of Himself. Are you mourning before God because you have not had an audible response? When you cannot hear God, you will find that He has trusted you in the most intimate way possible—with absolute *silence*, not a *silence* of despair, but one of pleasure, because He saw that you could withstand an even bigger revelation. If God has given you a *silence*, then praise Him—He is bringing you into the mainstream of His purposes. The actual evidence of the answer in time is simply a matter of God's sovereignty. Time is nothing to God. For a while you may have said, "I asked God to give me bread, but He gave me a stone instead" (see Matthew 7:9). He did not give you a stone, and today you find that

He gave you the "bread of life" (John 6:35).

A wonderful thing about God's *silence* is that His stillness is contagious—it gets into you, causing you to become perfectly confident so that you can honestly say, "I know that God has heard me." His *silence* is the very proof that He has. As long as you have the idea that God will always bless you in answer to prayer, He will do it, but He will never give you the grace of His *silence*. If Jesus Christ is bringing you into the understanding that prayer is for the glorifying of His Father, then He will give you the first sign of His intimacy—*silence*. (emphasis mine)[12]

Reflecting on the passage in John 11:6, Mary and Martha were hopeful that Jesus would come and make their brother Lazarus well. But Jesus did not come and make Lazarus well, but instead stayed where He was for another two days! And when Jesus finally made his way to Lazarus' tomb, what did He do instead of make him well? He raised him from the dead! Jesus was *silent* for two days and then He did a bigger miracle—raised Lazarus from the dead! This message of God's *silence* is so powerful to me!

This is what Mom was doing all this time...praying through the **Silence**, trusting God that *in His time* all would be well with Sarah, His child! Was it easy? No, it was not always easy! Was I always trusting? No, I was not always trusting! Did I become discouraged? Yes, many times! Did my faith falter? Yes, my faith did falter from time to time! But did I end each prayer and each day trusting God...and leaving Sarah in His hands? Yes, God gave me His peace to do just that! It took many long years of trusting and leaving her in His hands. It took many long years of God's *Silence*. But I can tell you that looking at her life today, there is no way I would have even *thought* of asking God for the way He has blessed her and given her the life she has today!

Thank you...thank you...thank you, God!

Chapter 28

"JUST KNOW I AM ALWAYS HERE!"

"I will never leave you nor forsake you!" Hebrews 13:5

Yes, I often was discouraged. My faith often faltered, but God never left me there! From time to time He would even show me in a very powerful way that He was very present...right there with me! Many times His touch in my life would not even involve Sarah, but it was only to tell *me*, "**I am here!**"

One powerful "God-touch" happened one evening in early December of 2001. Rich and I were at a church dinner in a downtown Minneapolis hotel. I have always been nervous about my cell phone when at a public event...*Did I turn it off? Am I sure I turned it off? I better check again!* We rode with friends to the dinner that evening, and I was especially conscious of turning my phone off before we even got to the dinner. I checked it again when we arrived. Yes, I was certain it was *off!* I could put my phone out of my mind, and I wouldn't have to worry about whether it was indeed off or not during the evening's program.

When the dinner and program were over and people were just visiting, I was sitting at a table chatting with someone when I heard a distant cell phone ring. I remember thinking that it was too bad someone had left their phone on and so good that it hadn't gone off during the program. Our friends were ready to leave, so I got up from the table and walked out of the room into the lobby area. As we were walking toward the escalator I heard the cell phone again. *Oh my goodness, it seemed to be coming from my purse! How could that be? Ringing from a cell phone that was turned off?* However, I reached into my purse, and sure enough, my phone was ringing! It was Sarah. "Mom, where are you? Grandpa fell and broke his hip, and he is at Fairview Hospital! I will wait until you get here...the doctors will wait to talk with you when you get here." We left immediately, and our friends dropped me off at the hospital.

Many, many times when I turn my cell phone off I forget to turn it back on. Sometimes I do not remember until hours later, and sometimes not until I plug it in to charge it at bedtime. I believe God could not take the chance that I might forget to turn it back on. He needed to get a message to me, so *He did it His way!* God turned on my cell phone so I could get Sarah's call in time to get to the hospital. Actually, Sarah *had* tried to call me several times before then and IT WAS NOT ON! God used my cell phone as another "touch of God" in my life to tell me, "**I am here!**"

Thank you...thank you...thank you, God!

There have been many "touches" like that in my life; some are just little things no one else would probably even notice, and some are too personal to share. But each of them was His powerful personal message to me…"**I AM HERE! I will never leave you nor forsake you!**"

Both Sarah and I knew that as she continued on, God would always be there…and continue on she did!

Chapter 29

"I THOUGHT I WAS GOING TO BE AN UNKNOWN PERSON IN A MORGUE!"

"For He orders His angels to protect you wherever you go." Psalms 91:11

When Sarah moved back to Minneapolis she began working again as a waitress and with the catering service. Once again, she moved to an apartment with friends; we began to see less and less of her as her life seemed to pick up where it had left off several years ago. Working as a waitress often meant working well into the night. On those nights, Sarah would have to walk alone to a parking lot in downtown Minneapolis very late at night or in the early morning hours. This Mom was very apprehensive about that part of Sarah's job. I can't tell you how very, very grateful I was that Sarah was willing to stay in touch with me during those times. She would call me on her cell phone when leaving the restaurant, once again when she had safely reached her car, and a final time as she was walking to her apartment. We would continue talking until she reached her apartment door and I knew she was safely inside. She always knew she could call me anytime on my cell phone…at any hour of the night (or morning). Once I knew she was safe, I could sleep in peace for the rest of the night.

Sarah knew that being a waitress and caterer was ultimately not what she wanted for the rest of her life. I knew she was continually struggling with her vision of the future; then one day she shared her thoughts with me. She planned to make an appointment with Miriam, her educational coach, with whom she had spent many hours during and after high school. I was thrilled to know that Sarah was ready to move in another direction. After several sessions with Miriam, Sarah's decision was to first go back to Landmark College for one semester and then on to Augsburg College in Minneapolis to finish the final semester needed for her degree. Sarah explained her decision in her application to return to Landmark.

> I want to come back to Landmark to strengthen my skills in a structured environment. My personal goal is to finish my degree. After attending Landmark ten years ago, I was confident and aware of my strengths and weaknesses. Ten years ago I should have capitalized on what I learned and continued on to finish school, but I didn't. I

went right into the work place. The last few years I have felt vulnerable, scared, unsure, and I question my ability to succeed. Coming back to Landmark will help me to concentrate on strengthening my ability to learn while understanding where my barriers of strengths and weaknesses lie. I want to find my confidence and self-esteem to succeed in my educational future. I am older and much wiser now and feel that attending Landmark now I will be able to take what I have learned, and will learn, and apply it toward my future education and my daily life.

With this as her goal, Sarah applied for another student loan and planned to head to Landmark College for the spring semester of 2002. In January, Sarah was on her way back to Landmark. This time she was driving a small brown Honda... alone! Mom was a "little" nervous, but it had nothing to do with her driving or her directions or finding her way around; Sarah always seemed to know where she was and had a wonderful sense of direction. I also knew that she was somewhat familiar with the East Coast and that the weather forecast was just fine. But moms worry about things like their children driving alone across the country. Sarah had made plans to stay with friends along the way, stopping at a friend's home in Chicago the first night and spending a night with a friend in New York before heading to Putney the following day.

She did tell me she would call me as soon as she arrived at Mark's home in New York. Even though it was never her idea, she always agreed to leave me with telephone numbers of her friends. Her plan was to get to Mark's house around ten that night, and she would call me as soon as she arrived.

Now it was midnight. Was it okay for Mom to be anxious? Because I was! I wondered if I dared call at midnight and upset Sarah if she was there and had just forgotten to call me. I decided to call. Mark's wife told me that Sarah in fact had not arrived yet, but she would be sure to have her call me when she did...and yes, they had been expecting her several hours ago too. I did not go to bed, but instead anxiously waited for the phone to ring. And I prayed: *Please, God, keep her safe.* The phone finally did ring at about 1 a.m. – Sarah had just arrived and had this tale to tell...

It was late, about 10 p.m., and Sarah was a little uncertain where she was supposed to get off the freeway to find the highway to Mark's. She was coming up to the Brooklyn Bridge and, while she was not sure if she was supposed to cross the bridge, she was fairly certain that the turn to Mark's was not on the other side of the bridge. So, she decided she had better take the last turn off the freeway before going over the Brooklyn Bridge. She turned off the freeway and immediately realized that she had taken a wrong turn... right into the middle of the Bronx of New York at 10:30 at night! She had no idea where she was or how to find her way out. As she drove for several blocks trying to orient herself, she noticed that men, both young and old, were lingering in groups on all the street corners. Having absolutely no idea where to go, she was, of course, beginning to panic! Instinctively, Sarah knew it would not be wise to stop and ask directions, but what should she do? She did not want to drive slowly, but she was lost, confused, and panicking... and she had no idea where to go.

Just as she was nervously pondering her course of action...BANG! She had just entered an intersection when another car ran through the red light, hit her car on the right fender, and promptly left the scene of the accident. WOW... she was stopped now! The next thing she knew, a middle-aged man was approaching her car. He indicated that he wanted to talk with her, so she turned down the window ever so slightly. (I can only imagine how very nervous she must have been!) This is what he told her in a very gentle and caring way: "You don't belong here. There is nothing wrong with your car, and I am going to tell you how to get out of here." And he did! He gave her explicit directions to get back to the bridge and over to the freeway! WOW...what a powerful and loving God we have!

Thank you...thank you...thank you, God!

When Sarah tells this story, she says that at the time she was driving, lost and confused, through the streets of the Bronx, all she kept thinking was that she was sure she would be an unknown person in a morgue in the Bronx...and no one would ever find her or know where she had gone!

By the time Sarah arrived at Mark's that night she was pretty shaken, but she did call me to assure me that she was safe. Late that night, across the miles, Sarah and I bowed our heads together and thanked our loving Heavenly Father for His protection that night. After I hung up the phone, I spent most of the rest of the night on my knees, praising and thanking God for His mighty hand of protection! And all I kept thinking was, *"For He orders His angels to protect you wherever you go."*

Chapter 30

CELEBRATING...FROM THE TOP!

"There are two things you can do when you come to a mountain: climb it or go around it. The second is the easiest, but you miss the view from the top!"
Author Unknown

*S*arah spent that spring semester at Landmark College. We were *so* proud of her as we read remarks from her professors there:

> "Sarah is an exceptional student, always working at the edge of her knowledge and skills."

> "Sarah has excelled in all areas of tutorial this semester."

> "Congratulations! You have achieved Dean's List for the spring 2002 semester. This is an outstanding accomplishment and reflects the care and effort you put into your work during the semester."

Do you remember that when Sarah entered Landmark College, she was reading at only a second-grade level? Well, after the five-week summer program at Landmark, Sarah was reading at the *seventh-grade level*...and when Sarah left Landmark College she was reading at the *college level!*

After completing that final semester at Landmark College, Sarah then returned home and made plans to finish her degree at Augsburg College in Minneapolis. She graduated from Augsburg College in May of 2003 with a degree in Communications, along with a double minor in Art and Sociology. It is impossible to put into words our emotions on that graduation day. My daughter—who at twenty-two years old was reading at only a second-grade level and who at that time had *never* read a full book—had earned a college degree!

And now it was time to CELEBRATE! We hosted an open house to which family and friends from near and far came to *celebrate* both Sarah's hard work and God's constant faithfulness, which had led to this accomplishment!

HELP US CELEBRATE!

SARAH'S GRADUATION
from
AUGSBURG COLLEGE

We are celebrating (from the top)!

*Perserverance...Determination...Courage...
Strength...Fulfilling a Dream!*

There are two things you can do
when you come to a mountain:
climb it or **go around it.**
The second is the easiest...
But you miss the view from the top!

Friends from all areas of Sarah's life came to our home that afternoon of the open house. Even though Sarah had stayed in touch with many of her school friends, they had not been to our home for a while. It was so fun for us to visit and connect with many of them again. Many grade-school friends—with whom I had sat around the table after school and chatted—were there. Several of them remarked, "Your house has not changed!" And it hadn't! Do you remember the friend who Sarah waited for to catch up with her at the Field Day relay in grade school? She was there, excited to be a part of this celebration. One of her friends took her little girl upstairs to see Sarah's pink "Marsha Brady" bedroom... which hadn't changed! Another was so excited to have her little son swing on the tire swing in the back yard, which was still there. And Mark...who called to tell me, "Sarah has been hit by a car!" Mark came from California to celebrate Sarah's graduation with us! Many friends from Sarah's "Ten Turbulent Years" were part of this celebration. And many of Sarah's adult friends and prayer warriors were with us to celebrate this event with overwhelming gratefulness and thanksgiving to God...the God who was with her on the mountain climb!

The amazing caterer, for whom Sarah worked and learned what I could never have taught her, became a very good friend to Sarah. She was so gracious to help me host this celebration. Her table setting and food presentation was spectacular. The celebration ended with many pictures of that memorable day!

While Sarah's graduation was by no means the end of her journey, it seemed to me that on the day that she received her college diploma, she had reached an important pinnacle. And again uppermost in my mind was the quote: "There are two things you can do when you come to a mountain: climb it or go around it. The second is the easiest...but you miss the view from the top!" What a courageous climb! Sarah could have taken the easy route; she could have given up when she felt, in her own words, "vulnerable, scared, [and] unsure." But she didn't give up. Instead, Sarah kept climbing until she reached her goal: a college degree. It was a formidable climb for both of us. Watching her accept her diploma was, for this mother, a definite "view from the top!" Sarah would have more goals in life and God does not intend anyone to *stay* forever on "the top." As Oswald Chambers writes, "It is in the valley that we have to live for the glory of God."[14] But, Sarah can now look at the rest of her life with amazing expectation since she has been on "the top" of this mountain with God.

WITH GOD'S HELP, SARAH REACHED
THE TOP!

Epilogue

"CAN I MARRY YOUR DAUGHTER?"

"God gives His best to those who leave the choice to Him."
Jim Elliot

*S*arah remained in Minneapolis to work and lived with a friend in a family-owned condo. While she was there she reconnected with many of the friends who had always been such an important part of her support team. And then, several years later, her life changed dramatically.

One morning in December, the telephone rang. "Mr. Holte, I'm calling to ask you if I can marry your daughter!" We certainly had been praying for that call, not knowing when it might come, but knowing we were very thrilled with the man Sarah had been dating. Larry was an incredible Christian man from a wonderful Christian family!

On July 19, 2008, Sarah and Larry were married. The wedding was in Chicago and attended by family and an amazing number of friends from all over the country.

And now I could include my new son-in-law in the prayer

that I pray for each of my family members every day…

Lord, thank you for giving her/him…
Your peace…Your strength…Your love…
Your protection…Your joy…Your wisdom…
And Your forgiveness.

Currently, Sarah and Larry are happily married and living in Chicago. I believe one of the biggest blessings a parent can experience is to continue to have a close relationship after a child's marriage…with your child as well as her spouse. And in this we are truly blessed! Sarah calls us often—just to stay in touch—and her husband many times will say, "I haven't talked with your mom and dad lately…let's call them!" We are so grateful to also have this close relationship with our other two daughters and their families. Thank you, God!

We have also discovered that we now are a part of another "family." We consider Larry's extended family…"family"… and in turn we are considered "family" by them. We worship together, we eat together, we shop together, we have fun together…we even watch TV together! We are always welcome in their home! We are included in any special event in their family.

Thank you…thank you…thank you, God!

Sarah is a confident, competent, forward-looking girl with many interests and possibilities in her future. This mother trusts and, from experience, knows that God will be with her as she confronts any new challenges in her life ahead.

GREAT IS HIS FAITHFULNESS!

ADDITIONAL MATERIAL

The Importance of Friends in the Lives of Those Struggling
    with Dyslexia and Attention Deficit Disorder (ADD)

What Exactly is Dyslexia and Attention Deficit Disorder
(ADD)?

Can a Dyslexic be Successful in Life?

Recommended Resources

Landmark College Information

In Sarah's Own Words

What More Can I Say?

THE IMPORTANCE OF FRIENDS IN THE LIVES OF THOSE STRUGGLING WITH DYSLEXIA AND ATTENTION DEFICIT DISORDER (ADD)

*T*his book has been a witness to *faith* as the strength for living through the many years of dyslexia and attention deficit disorder (ADD). But along with *faith*, I cannot ignore the powerful impact of friends and family during these years of struggle. The support of our family and many friends was a blessing which kept us going each day. In his book *The Misunderstood Child,* Dr. Larry Silver emphasizes the importance of a strong support system for a person with learning disabilities, saying that it is the most important need of a learning-disabled individual.[15]

Friends were of utmost importance in Sarah's life from early on and to this day. God somehow revealed to me early in Sarah's life how important it was to keep her connected to friends both young and old.

It was not until I began writing this book did I realize the impact of this decision on Sarah's life. Friends are important in any of our lives, but I am convinced that this is an essential factor in the life of a child with learning disabilities or attention deficit disorder (ADD). I am only a mother, not a professional, but I believe that learning to relate to others, friends in particular, early in the life of a child with learning disabilities or attention deficit disorder (ADD) is so very important. A child with a learning disability or attention deficit disorder (ADD) may act out or interact with other children in a way that would cause them to shun the learning-disabled child. This is devastating to a child.

Again, only as a mother, I believe it is the parent that must be proactive early in a child's life to consciously provide opportunities for the child to be involved with other children. It is important for the parent to be aware of the interaction of his/her child with other children. Coaching the child in relating to others will make a huge difference in later years. I believe that providing these relational opportunities early in a child's life will enable the child to begin to learn from others, as well as how his/her behavior affects the other children either positively or negatively. Engaging in conversation with others as a child grows enables the child to learn how to communicate and to be comfortable in conversation as they relate to others. As the child gathers more and more friends around him/her, these children begin to bond and accept one another just the way they are. All of this builds confidence in the learning-disabled child as he/she grows older and interacts with more and more children. And as proven in Sarah's life, as she grew older her friends were always there for her no matter what her grades were or how "distracted" she may have been.

Providing opportunities for a child to be connected to adults as well will be immensely important as the child becomes older. Not only will the child be comfortable around adults and learn to communicate with them, but this connection will provide valuable support in his/her future life.

It was also important for *me* to be connected with *Sarah's* friends, and for *her* to be connected with *the parents* of her friends. The circle of friends that surrounded Rich and me became her friends and support as well. From time to time, I would send a note to friends and family, either requesting their prayer or thanking them for their support. I am confident Sarah felt the love and support of these friends and that God used them powerfully in her years of struggling.

We are so blessed to be able to maintain our connection with this group of friends...both parents and children alike. A number of Sarah's friends have moved away, but we as parents continue to stay connected and have a very special bond with each other and our children. We are *very, very* grateful for these friends and family in our life.

The following note was sent with Sarah's high school graduation picture as a thank you:

To the Parents of our Daughter's Friend,

We are grateful to you for touching our daughter's life! Whether you have known Sarah for one year or ten years or eighteen years, whether she spent little or lots of time in your presence, whether you were aware of it or not—you have made an impact on her life and contributed to who she is today. And we want to say "thank you" for that! We thank you for your caring and support. We are grateful for the values you hold and your willingness to take a stand. We are grateful for your faith and your eagerness to share it. We thank you for your example, your consistency, your understanding, and your forgiveness. We thank you for being her friend. We thank you for your interest in her. We thank you for opening your home and very often your kitchen! We thank you for your expression of love to her in so many different and special ways. And more than anything we thank you for sharing your daughter/son.

Sarah has been a joy in our lives for eighteen years and now she will move on to build her own little world in a new way. She will be strong and secure, in part, because of your touch in her life. We have released her into God's hands and just thank Him for bringing such special people into her life. Bless you!

And this note was sent before sending Sarah off for her freshman year at Westmont College.

Dear friend,

Would you be willing to include Sarah in your daily prayers? Because of her reading disability, this next year at Westmont without a tutor will be a real challenge. Specifically, she will need to be able to:

1. Get through huge volumes of reading material for each class.
2. Comprehend what she is reading.
3. Put together her thoughts from the reading material in the form of writing and speaking.
4. Assimilate and remember those thoughts for answering questions and taking tests.
5. Stay close and draw upon the wisdom and strength of her heavenly Father.

Sarah will be taking these classes the first semester: English Composition, New Testament Studies, Public Speaking, and Physical Fitness.

Knowing that she is being held up in prayer by family and friends will be such an encouragement to her—and, we believe, follows Jesus' command to "ask and ye shall receive" according to His will.

Thank you for lifting up Sarah in both petition and thanksgiving. We are truly blessed with faithful family and friends! Bless you!

And the following was included in Sarah's college graduation announcement:

To Sarah's support team and prayer warriors!

We are convinced that the culmination of this dream in Sarah's life is due to several key factors in her life:

- Sarah's tutor Elayne: for her early intervention, constant care and concern...and for always being there!
- Dr. Abuzzahab: for his wise evaluation and skill in prescribing medication for Sarah's dyslexia and attention deficit disorder (ADD).
- Landmark College and staff: for their dedication and commitment to an absolutely incredible educational model for learning-disabled students.
- Dear family and friends: for overwhelming support in prayer and love

and who just never forgot her.

- And finally, Sarah herself: for her courage, determination, and faith in a loving God who has touched her life in so many miraculous ways!

Friends, we thank you deeply for your love and support and prayers. Your interest and care have been such an encouragement to all of us. Thank you for your touch in Sarah's life!

WHAT EXACTLY IS DYSLEXIA AND ATTENTION DEFICIT DISORDER (ADD)?

What are the professional definitions of dyslexia and attention deficit disorder (ADD), and what do the experts say about these disabilities? I will be unable, within the scope of this book, to provide all the technical information about learning disabilities, but I can provide references and quote several definitions from professional writings.

Dyslexia:

The International Dyslexia Association (IDA) provides some excellent information regarding dyslexia, including their formal definition of this learning disability:

> Dyslexia is a specific learning disability that is neurological in origin. It is characterized by difficulties with accurate and/or fluent word recognition and by poor spelling and decoding abilities. These difficulties typically result from a deficit in the phonological component of language that is often unexpected in relation to other cognitive abilities and the provision of effective classroom instruction. Secondary

consequences may include problems in reading comprehension and reduced reading experience that can impede growth of vocabulary and background knowledge. Studies show that individuals with dyslexia process information in a different area of the brain than do non-dyslexics. Many people who are dyslexic are of average to above average intelligence.[16]

One of the first professionals I heard talk with parents and educators on the subject of learning disabilities was Larry Silver, MD. At the time, Dr. Silver was a clinical professor of psychiatry at Georgetown University Medical Center. Dr. Silver was the speaker at the conference on dyslexia that Sarah attended in California, and it was he who prompted the telephone call about the summer program at Landmark College. At that conference, Sarah was excited to hear about the possibilities at Landmark, but what she heard from Dr. Silver about her learning disability was the real life-changing moment—in both her life and mine! She brought home a tape from the conference of Dr. Silver's message titled "The Misunderstood Child." I listened to that tape over and over again for the next ten years, and I went to any conference where he was going to be speaking. His message had so many answers and was so healing! He has since written a book also titled *The Misunderstood Child*.

In Dr. Silver's book, he addresses the nature of dyslexia in the chapter titled "What You Must Know to Understand

Learning Disabilities." He explains that learning disabilities are disorders of the brain in which it is "wired" in a different way than normal. Dr. Silver stresses that the brain of a learning-disabled person is not defective or damaged, but rather just different.[17]

I must also address what dyslexia is NOT, as there are many myths and misconceptions surrounding this learning disability. One of the greatest misconceptions about dyslexics is that "dyslexia is associated with low intelligence and low cognitive ability,"[18] however, this is absolutely NOT true. Rather, to quote the International Dyslexia Association:

> There is no correlation between dyslexia, a brain-based heritable learning disorder, and intelligence. In fact, there are many adults who have *above average intellectual abilities and talents* that enable them to compensate for weak reading skills *(emphasis mine)*.[19]

Another common misconception about dyslexia is that it is untreatable, but as this book testifies, I know from experience that this is certainly NOT true!

Attention Deficit Disorder (ADD):

One of the most common questions regarding attention deficit disorder (ADD) is whether it is the same as "attention deficit *hyperactivity* disorder" (AD/HD). According to the Attention Deficit Disorder Association, the 'official' term is actually attention deficit hyperactivity disorder (AD/HD), of which there are several different types, but the term "attention deficit disorder," or often simply "ADD," is often used to refer to all types of AD/HD—even among professionals.[20]

Just like dyslexia, attention deficit disorder (ADD) is also a neurobiological disorder. Attention deficit disorder is characterized by inappropriate inattention and impulsiveness. Though most people may at times have trouble paying attention or controlling their impulses, for people with attention deficit disorder (ADD) the problem interferes with almost every aspect of their lives.[21]

Attention deficit disorder (ADD) is not a learning disability, but rather is labeled as a behavioral disorder. However, the International Dyslexia Association addresses the fact that it is quite common for those with learning disabilities to also have an attention deficit disorder (ADD):

> In various studies as many as 50% of those diagnosed with a learning or reading [disability] have also been diagnosed with AD/HD. Although disabilities may co-occur, one is not the cause of the other.[22]

Just as I did with dyslexia, I also want to address some of the myths surrounding attention deficit hyperactivity disorder (AD/HD), namely that it is NOT caused by too much sugar or TV, nor by failure on the part of parents or teachers.[23] Attention deficit disorder (ADD) is not, in fact, caused by any external factors, but rather by abnormal brain activity.

CAN A DYSLEXIC BE
SUCCESSFUL IN LIFE?

his book would not be complete without addressing a common question that is often in the back of the minds of those unfamiliar with dyslexia, that is: "Can someone with dyslexia be successful in life?" An article about successful dyslexics quotes this:

"Many [dyslexics] have been outstanding in their fields. Examples of successful dyslexics are: Nelson Rockefeller, Woodrow Wilson, Winston Churchill, Albert Einstein, General Patton, Bruce Jenner, Thomas Edison, and William Butler Yeats. The intelligence of some of these men was in the upper stratum, yet many—early in their lives—were judged to be "uneducable" or even "idiot." Others, although not world-famous, have been successful in business, mechanical fields, architecture, the arts, and other career areas. Some have become doctors, scientists, inventors, politicians, and generals. Some have become highly creative problem solvers. Most of these people have never excelled in reading and have remained poor spellers."[24]

In my own further research I also found these "famous" people with the gift of dyslexia: Charles Schwab, William Hewlett, Ted Turner, Walt Disney, Tommy Hilfiger, Attorney David Boies, Tom Cruise, Henry Winkler, and Loretta Young.

RECOMMENDED RESOURCES

*A*s a mother of a child with a learning disability and attention deficit disorder (ADD), I found that to help my child function in life, it was critical for me to understand everything possible about these disabilities. I believe it is essential to seek out information and be current on all there is to know about these disabilities.

Books:

Cole, David and Jonathan Mooney. *Learning Outside the Lines: Two Ivy League Students with Learning Disabilities and ADHD Give You Tools for Academic Success and Educational Revolution*. New York: Simon & Schuster, 2000.

Hallowell, Edward M. and John J. Ratey. *Delivered from Distraction: Getting the Most Out of Life with Attention Deficit Disorder*. New York: Ballantine Books, 2005.

Hallowell, Edward M. and John J. Ratey. *Driven to*

Distraction: Recognizing and Coping with Attention Deficit Disorder from Childhood through Adulthood. New York: Touchstone, 1995.

Kelly, Kate and Peggy Ramundo. *You Mean I'm Not Lazy, Stupid, or Crazy?! A Self-Help Book for Adults with Attention Deficit Disorder.* New York: Scribners, 1995.

Kolberg, Judith and Kathleen G. Nadeau. *ADD-Friendly Ways to Organize Your Life: Strategies that Work from a Professional Organizer and a Renowned ADD Clinician.* New York: Routledge Taylor & Francis Group, 2002.

Lavoie, Richard. *It's So Much Work to be Your Friend: Helping the Child with Learning Disabilities Find Social Success.* New York: Simon & Schuster, 2005.

Nadeau, Kathleen G. and Patricia O. Quinn. *Understanding Women with AD/HD.* Washington, D.C.: Advantage Books, 2002.

Ratey, Nancy A. *The Disorganized Mind: Coaching Your ADHD Brain to Take Control of Your Time, Tasks, and Talents.* New York: St. Martin's Press, 2008.

Silver, Larry B. *Dr. Larry Silver's Advice to Parents on*

ADHD. New York: Three Rivers Press, 1999.

Silver, Larry B. *The Misunderstood Child: Understanding and Coping with Your Child's Learning Disability*, 4th Edition. New York: Three Rivers Press, 2006.

Solden, Sari. *Women with Attention Deficit Disorder: Embracing Disorganization at Home and in the Workplace*. Grass Valley, CA: Underwood Books, 1995.

Weiss, Lynn. *ADD on the Job: Making Your ADD Work for You*. Lanham: Taylor Trade Publishing, 1996.

Ziegler Dendy, Chris A. *Teaching Teens with ADD and ADHD: A Quick Reference Guide for Teachers and Parents*. Bethesda: Woodbine House, 2000.

Websites:

Attention Deficit Disorder Association: *www.add.org*

Children and Adults with ADD: *www.chadd.org*

International Dyslexia Association: *www.interdys.org*

Landmark College: *www.landmark.edu*

LANDMARK COLLEGE
INFORMATION

The following information was provided by Landmark College to include in this book:

Landmark College –
A Unique Postsecondary Institution
Serving a Distinctive Student Population

Landmark's strength and its unique competencies and expertise derive from three main sources. The first is nearly three decades of direct experience working with students with diagnosed learning and attention differences at the point of the college transition and in a rigorous post-secondary framework. In this time over 10,000 such students have experienced Landmark's distinctive programs.

Every dimension of the College's academic, residential, co-curricular, support, and other programs has been designed expressly to serve the needs of these students. No other institution in the world can claim this depth of experience, and what we have learned in the process has unique and immeasurable value for the world of education in general.

This experience is made particularly valuable by the fact that for more than the past two decades Landmark has pursued a dual mission, in which its internal activities for the students who attend programs on the Putney, VT, campus have served as a teaching-learning laboratory for an external dimension of the mission—focused on training educators and improving educational systems, programs, and curricula across the country and around the world. This second source of organizational strength and depth—the external dimension of Landmark's mission—is not an add-on, it is central to our focus as a post-secondary organization. Since the late 1980s we have provided training and consultation to thousands of educators and hundreds of high schools, colleges, and universities. For a small, young College we have demonstrated an extraordinary track record of winning federal and state grants to augment the development of our knowledge, to establish empirically-validated Best Practices, and to disseminate this knowledge to other institutions, while also providing fee-based consultative services and professional development programming, including graduate-level, hybrid, and online certificate programs.

The third source of Landmark's unique power as an educational program and as a partner to other institutions is related to this integration of internal programs and practices and an outward focus, in which what we learn and develop in Putney is validated by its expression and implementation in external contexts, and what we learn from the process of disseminating our knowledge in turn informs our internal development. Landmark College is a comprehensive educational system, in which every dimension of the College's activities supports the development and provision of research-based programs, curricula, and teaching approaches that have demonstrated their worth for countless students and that have proven equally valuable in a broad range of external educational environments.

Landmark's core programs are uniquely powerful. Each year well over a hundred students who had struggled in high school or failed out of college elsewhere graduate from our Associate's degree programs and go on to succeed in four-year colleges of their choice. Recently, other students have begun the challenging journey to attaining a B.A. degree at the College, after a successful substantive change application was accepted by our regional accreditors. Countless other students take advantage of short-term programs or a semester or two in our system and also go on to far better educational outcomes than they had previously experienced. Our program as a whole is unreplicable—in part because of its complexity and labor-intensiveness, and in part because our experience of ongoing development during a time when the LD field itself has gone through deep and far-reaching advances in its understanding of learning disorders and effective educational systems and practices can truly not be duplicated. At the same time, virtually every aspect of our internal program can be modified and delivered in other contexts, and through the external dimension of our mission, that is precisely what Landmark has delivered in an increasingly broad array of institutional settings.

Ten years ago, the *Wall Street Journal* wrote that "no one knows the business of educating students with learning disabilities better than Landmark College." That is even more the case today. That this is so is because of the comprehensive and systematic approach we have taken to our development as an educational system focused on influencing educational practices on the broadest scale. Even more so, it is so because, as we have worked with thousands of students and developed unprecedented experience and expertise, we have continually been open to new developments in the field and to input from the larger world. The outcome is the most robust and capable teaching environment on the planet, one designed to support the most complex learners in the world during their journey to academic and life success.

Dr. Brent Betit, Senior Vice President
Landmark College

About Landmark College

When you think about it, everyone recognizes that people are different from each other. Not everyone listens to the same music. Not everyone appreciates the same art. Not everyone is good at the same sport. And not everyone learns the same way!

Our Mission

Landmark College's mission is to transform the way students learn, educators teach, and the public thinks about education. We provide highly accessible approaches to learning that empower individuals who learn differently to exceed their aspirations and to achieve their greatest potential. Through the Landmark College Institute for Research and Training, the College aims to extend its mission across the nation and throughout the world.

Degrees and Programs

Landmark College is a collaborative community, fully committed to serving students who learn differently. Whether a student is ready to pursue a bachelor's degree, someone who loves business, life sciences, or computer science and gaming, and wants to study in these fields, or is excited about earning an associate degree, Landmark College could be the right fit. The College offers summer and January term programs, both on-campus and through study abroad. Many programs are for both current and visiting college students, and there are several options for high school students as well. At Landmark, everyone is focused on helping students achieve their goals and discover their paths as confident, empowered, and independent learners.

Why Landmark?

If you're a bright, talented, college-bound student with a learning disability, ADHD, or ASD—or if you are in college and struggling with a learning disability—we invite you to discover why so many students are choosing Landmark College *(www.landmark.edu/ admissions/for-students)*.

For more information, visit Landmark College's website:

www.landmark.edu

IN SARAH'S OWN WORDS

This book would also not be complete without hearing a small piece of Sarah's story in her own words. In the following pages, I will share several of Sarah's papers that she had written during the years of her journey to the top.

Essay written about Westmont College (1989):

In the three years I attended Westmont God really blessed me, challenged me, and constantly kept me growing in my faith. I grew as an individual and in my faith.

There are many positive qualities Westmont holds. I feel that the strongest quality Westmont has to offer is the faith and learning from professors and faculty. It is something to be valued, which is often taken for granted. They are living testimonies that have really encouraged me as a person, and mostly as a Christian. I didn't realize how much they had impacted my life until this semester away from Westmont.

I also really enjoyed and treasure the interaction of faith and learning at Westmont. It is an important part of their teaching, whether it be in the lecture hall or in their offices. The students have also greatly influenced my life and continue to do so even though I am absent from them. The Christian environment is a very supportive and encouraging place to learn, as well as to grow spiritually. The relationships I formed during my three years at Westmont have become my lifeline and will continue to be a vital part of my life.

Personal Statement written for Augsburg College Application (1989):

An achievement in my life which resulted in a personal satisfaction was my struggle to overcome my learning disability. When I was in ninth grade I discovered that I had the ability to read and write of a second-grader. At that point in my life I had to make a choice either to give it my all and try to overcome it, or to throw it all away and give up completely. I was ready to throw it all away, for trying to achieve this high of a goal would mean lots of sacrifices. Talking to my tutor, she encouraged me to continue on with tutoring.

Throughout the years I struggled very much. I remember times crying all night, crying, wanting to wake up from this bad dream. Throughout all these hard times I still continued to see my tutor. During the summer, I was going four times a week for an hour and then when school started I continued to see her for three times a week for an hour. After a year I was able to understand more the way I learned and how I need to learn. Through learning this and being able to apply this to my learning style, it came easier for me. I was able to admit I had a problem and had to live with it. In my junior year I progressed a lot, especially in my writing and reading skills, and I brought my grades up.

But during my senior year, I became somewhat discouraged because I felt I should be overcoming this disability with my tutoring help. I felt helpless and confused, and I didn't understand until my tutor told me I'll always have to live with this learning disability. I will always have to work hard, even harder than I did in high school. Through this rough experience I went through, and still am and always will, I am able to look back and see how much progress I have made and how much more I am learning every day. On graduation day I said to myself, "If I can get through this, I can get through anything else that's put in my way."

Another thing I learned from this experience is that a person needs a goal in life. In order to achieve that goal one must be persistent and never give up working toward that goal. I believe this because I know I can achieve, at least to some degree, anything I'm determined to do.

Paper written for a class at Landmark (1991)

The education system for my parents has been very frustrating and heartbreaking, and for me it has been extremely confusing and scary.

My mother sensed something way back in first grade when I began the year in the top reading group and ended the year in the bottom reading group. And it went downhill from there.

Some of my test results here at Landmark show I am right now at an eight-year-old and ten-year-old reading level, and yet up to this point I have never been identified as learning disabled by any school system (either public or private), nor have I had any special education classes in any of the schools I have attended. I have had very extensive testing and private tutoring since I was in tenth grade, only because my parents were convinced I needed it.

When I was in elementary school, my parents rarely saw my papers on display when they visited school...they were not written well enough to be put on the board. My spelling papers were never put up because I didn't get perfect papers. I was never given a part in any school performance—little plays or other things for parents—because those parts were always for the kids that did well in school. I was not chosen for anything special because, again, only the kids that did well in school had those honors. As younger kids we always looked forward to being a school patrol when we got to be sixth graders. But (and I didn't know this), my teacher had decided not to allow me to be a patrol because of my poor school perfor- mance...until my mother went to the school and cried, telling them I was certainly just as responsible and could handle the job as well as any of the other students. (I didn't even know this until just this year when my mother told me what she had done.) My sixth grade teacher was perhaps the most unsympathetic. Most of my papers would come back with big red markings all over: "CARELESS! THIS WAS IN NO CONDITION TO HAND IN!! POORLY ORGANIZED!! IF YOU HAD PROOFREAD YOU WOULD HAVE BEEN ABLE TO TELL IT DIDN'T MAKE ANY SENSE!! YOU MAKE THESE ERRORS OVER AND OVER AGAIN!!" And always: "PROOFREAD, PROOFREAD, PROOFREAD!!" in BIG read letters (and, of course, proofreading would do no good, because it looked good to me the first time and looked just as right when I re-read it). I was reprimanded over and over again, but never did anyone take the time to try to help me do a better job.

My mother was at the school three or four times a year during elementary school, begging them to give me some help, but was always told that she just could not accept an average child and that often I just did not care enough to do a good job. They continually said I was "just careless." I always had many friends and was very social; in fact, my friends were always the high achievers in school. I guess I just did not fit the mold of a learning-disabled child.

Junior high school was very bad (I don't believe that in elementary school I even realized that I did things differently from my friends). My teachers there had even less patience and certainly no time at all for someone who was "not willing to put any effort into her school work." I changed public schools, but that didn't help. Nobody took the time to ask any questions or offer any help.

In ninth grade my parents sent me to a private high school (and I went under protest!!). Classes were smaller, some teachers were more concerned, but still it was always me that didn't put in the effort to be successful. Teachers would tell my parents that I was always daydreaming, not paying attention: "she doesn't follow directions...doesn't stay at a task...doesn't care." I got through high school only by going to a wonderful private tutor three times a week; she made me feel good about myself even though I was not successful in school. She helped me to understand my learning style and understand that I had many other strengths. But by that time it was too late to try to remediate but only to help me maintain my current subjects. I graduated from high school fourth from the bottom of my class. But my parents were proud of my accomplishment!

I was accepted at a small Christian college in California. I believe I was accepted because I convinced them that I wanted to learn and I would give my best with some help from the school.

Essay written about Landmark College (1992):

Landmark not only gave me the ability to understand my dyslexia, but through the study skills process, I gained the freedom to learn. I was given the tools to read, to write, and actually understand what I was reading and writing. For the first time I gained the confidence to speak my opinions and to ask others "Why?" I suddenly had a craving for knowledge. There is no way to express the caring, the patience, and the commitment that each teacher gives his/her students. I remember during the Summer Program in 1990 sitting in my tutorial two times a day for two to three days just learning about vowels. I asked my teacher, "Don't you just want to strangle me?" I just didn't get it! Well, I finally did! And then I remember thinking one day, *This outline thing is pretty handy... why didn't anyone share this idea with me in high school and college?* (Or maybe they did, and I was too busy listening to everything else going on around me!)

I treasure my experience at Landmark and I deeply treasure the friendships and bonds that I formed. I learned about life there. For the first time I played fruit bowling, got up at 5 a.m. to study, skied in Sugar Bush, drove 45 miles for a Taco Bell, videotaped an entire weekend (which could damage any chances for a political career), did random "whatever" polls, studied until 3 a.m., walked 50+ blocks in New York City, woke up at 4:30 a.m. to take the train into "the city" and see Wall Street and the people who work there, see what they look like and how they dress, ate in an igloo, went "shooting" with 19 dyslexics, learned the true meaning of procrastination, and got my room dusted with baby powder.

Given this opportunity to share my feelings about Landmark, I would like to end by thanking everyone at Landmark for inspiring me and believing in me...you really *did* change my life!

Personal Statement written for Landmark College Application (2001):

My educational experience has been a

rough road at times. In high school I really struggled to just stay afloat and get by. I didn't understand why or what was happening. I barely got by. In college, I got by because I had wonderful friends who helped me get through my classes. I am not really sure how I made it through three years. In the middle of my third year it all hit me. I had a meltdown. I felt overwhelmed, confused and frustrated. I didn't understand why I couldn't "get it!" I then found Landmark College in 1990 and my whole world opened up. I began to see the light at the end of the tunnel. I began to understand my strengths and weaknesses better. I am a visual learner. I always learn best through pictures. My weaknesses are vocabulary, pronunciation, concentrating and focusing.

I want to come back to Landmark to strengthen my skills in a structured environment. I want to focus my attention on continuing my education. My personal goal is to finish my degree. After attending Landmark ten years ago, I was confident and aware of my strengths and weaknesses. Ten years ago I should have capitalized on what I learned and continued on to finish school, but I didn't. I went right into the work place. The last few years I have felt vulnerable, scared, unsure, and I question my ability to succeed. Coming back to Landmark will help me to concentrate on strengthening my ability to learn while understanding where my barriers of strengths and weaknesses lie. I want to find my confidence and self-esteem to succeed in my educational future. I am older and much wiser now and feel that attending Landmark now I will be able to take what I have learned, and will learn, and apply it toward my future education and my daily life.

WHAT MORE CAN I SAY?

s I complete this book of Sarah's and my "journey to the top" and ask myself the question, "What more can I say?," I have nothing more to "say" other than to share once again some of the words that helped me face each new day during those years of struggling…and each new day since.

Here are several more quotes from my torn and tattered book *My Utmost for His Highest* by Oswald Chambers:

> "A child of God never prays to be made aware of the fact that God answers prayer, because he is so restfully certain that God always answers prayer."[25]

> "The purpose of prayer is that we get ahold of God, not of the answer."[26]

> "Unless you learn to open the door of your life completely and let God in from your first waking moment of each new day, you will be working on the wrong level throughout the

day. But if you will swing the door of your life fully open and 'pray to your Father who is in the secret place,' every public thing in your life will be marked with the lasting imprint of the presence of God."[27]

The following are selections from my other torn and tattered book *Come Away My Beloved* by Frances J. Roberts. Each selection is an excerpt from a longer piece (the title of which you can find in the end notes):

> "O My children, what do you need today? Is it comfort; is it courage; is it healing; is it guidance? Lo, I say unto thee, that whatever it is ye need, if you will look to Me, I will supply."[28]

> "My child, I have loved thee simply because I have loved thee, and what need I of any other reason; Shall I not shed My love upon thee for no other reason than simply that I have chosen so to do?"[29]

> "O My child, give Me your mind. I shall keep it in perfect tranquility. Give Me your thoughts; I will keep them in peace."[30]

> "Behold, in the hollow of My hand, there have

I made thee a nest, and thou shalt lay thee down and sleep. Yea, I have begotten thee, I have called thee by name, and thou art Mine. I have not taken thee out of the world, but I am with thee to help thee and to encourage thee, and to give thee strength in all thou shalt be called upon to endure. Thou facest each new day with Me at thy side. (Never forget that I am there.) Thou meetest every difficult circumstance with Mine arm outstretched to fight for thee."[31]

"Tarry not for an opportunity to have more time to be alone with Me. Take it, though ye leave the tasks at hand. Nothing will suffer. Things are of less importance than ye think."[32]

"My promises are of no avail to thee except as ye apply and appropriate them by faith. In thy daily walk, ye shall be victorious only to the degree that ye trust Me. I can help thee only as ye ask. I shall meet you at every point where ye put action alongside thy prayers. Only as ye walk shall the waters of adversity be parted before thee."[33]

"For though you have forgotten Me, I have not forgotten you. Whilst ye have busied yourselves with your daily occupations, I have still been occupied with you. When your mind has been captured by the affairs of life, My thoughts have been of you."[34]

"There is never a day, there is never an hour, there is never a moment when you are outside My thought."[35]

"Praise Me. This I ask of thee in times when it seemeth indescribably difficult to do so. I ask it of thee in love that is stern at this point because I know unequivocally that it is your only hope for survival. Distress of soul and grief of heart can only bring on destruction of body. Joy alone is a healer, and ye can have it in the darkest hour if ye will force thy soul to rise to Me in worship and adoration."[36]

The following are some of my favorite passages that give me strength and peace:

"How precious it is, Lord, to realize that you are thinking about me constantly! I can't even count how many times a day your thoughts turn towards me. And when I wake in the morning, you are thinking of me!" *Psalms 139:17-18*

"He is the God who keeps every promise."
Psalms 146:6b

"Jehovah Himself is caring for you." *Psalms 121:5*

"The Lord will work out His plans for my life." *Psalms 138:8a*

"You alone are my God; my times are in Your hands." *Psalms 31:15*

"Every morning tell Him, "Thank you for your kindness," and every evening rejoice in all His faithfulness." *Psalms 92:2*

"Touch not these chosen ones of Mine." *Psalms 105:15*

"He would not let one thing be done to them apart from His decision." *Psalms 105:14*

"Why am I praying like this? Because I know you will answer me, O God." *Psalms 17:6*

"What time I am afraid, I will trust in Thee." *Psalms 56:3 (KJV)*

"I will make my people strong with power from me. They will go wherever they wish, and wherever they go, they will be under My personal care." *Zechariah 10:12*

And lastly, here are several hymns that have strengthened me along this journey:

"Take Time to be Holy"
(words by William D. Longstaff, 1882)

Take time to be holy, speak oft with thy Lord
Abide in Him always, and feed on His Word
Make friends of God's children
Help those who are weak
Forgetting in nothing His blessing to seek

Take time to be holy, the world rushes on
Spend much time in secret with Jesus along
By looking to Jesus, like Him thou shalt be
Thy friends in thy conduct His likeness shall see

Take time to be holy, let Him be thy Guide
And run not before Him, whatever betide
In joy or in sorrow, still follow thy Lord
And looking to Jesus, still trust in His Word

Take time to be holy, be calm in thy soul
Each thought and each motive, beneath His control
Thus led by His Spirit, to fountains of love
Thou soon shalt be fitted, for service above

"Standing on the Promises of God"
(words by R. Kelso Carter, 1886)

Standing on the promises of Christ my King
Through eternal ages let His praises ring
Glory in the highest, I will shout and sing
Standing on the promises of God

Standing on the promises that cannot fail
When the howling storms of doubt and fear assail
By the living Word of God I shall prevail
Standing on the promises of God

Standing on the promises I cannot fail
Listening every moment to the Spirit's call
Resting in my Savior, as my all in all
Standing on the promises of God

What more can I say? Only this:

TO GOD BE THE GLORY!

END NOTES

1. Boltz, Ray. "Give Me Your Hand." © 2002. Used By Permission of Ray Boltz/Shepherd Boy Music.

2. Roberts, Frances J. "I Will Bring the Victory." *Come Away My Beloved, Updated Version.* Uhrichsville, OH: Barbour Publishing, Inc., 2002. Page 57. Used with permission of Barbour Publishing, Inc.

3. Though the official clinical diagnosis is "attention deficit *hyperactivity* disorder (AD/HD)," the term "attention deficit disorder (ADD)" is more widely used among the general public as well as generally accepted among professionals. For consistency's sake, I will refer to this disorder as "attention deficit disorder (ADD)" throughout the book.

4. Roberts, Frances J. "Learn to Reign." *Come Away My Beloved.* Uhrichsville, OH: Barbour Publishing, Inc., 1973. Page 168. Used with permission of Barbour Publishing, Inc.

5. Winstead, Trudy. "Thy Name is Courage." Used with permission of Trudy Winstead.

6. Ibid.

7. Solden, Sari. *Women and Attention Deficit Disorder Embracing Disorganization at Home and in the Workplace.* Grass Valley, CA: Underwood Books, 1995.

8. Boltz, Ray. "Give Me Your Hand." © 2002. Used By Permission of Ray Boltz/Shepherd Boy Music.

9. Chambers, Oswald. "Nothing of the Old Life!" (October 23). Taken from *My Utmost for His Highest* by Oswald Chambers, edited by James Reimann, © 1992 by Oswald Chambers Publications Assn., Ltd., and used by permission of Discovery House Publishers, Grand Rapids, MI 49501. All rights reserved.

10. Chambers, Oswald. "The Teaching of Adversity" (August 2). Taken from *My Utmost for His Highest* by Oswald Chambers, edited by James Reimann, © 1992 by Oswald Chambers Publications Assn., Ltd., and used by permission of Discovery House Publishers, Grand Rapids, MI 49501. All rights reserved.

11. Chambers, Oswald. "The Overshadowing of God's Personal Deliverance" (June 27). Taken from *My Utmost for His Highest* by Oswald Chambers, edited

by James Reimann, © 1992 by Oswald Chambers Publications Assn., Ltd., and used by permission of Discovery House Publishers, Grand Rapids, MI 49501. All rights reserved.

12. Chambers, Oswald. "God's Silence—Then What?" (October 11). Taken from *My Utmost for His Highest* by Oswald Chambers, edited by James Reimann, © 1992 by Oswald Chambers Publications Assn., Ltd., and used by permission of Discovery House Publishers, Grand Rapids, MI 49501. All rights reserved.

13. Boltz, Ray. "Another Child to Hold." © 1991. Used By Permission of Ray Boltz/Shepherd Boy Music.

14. Chambers, Oswald. "The Place of Humiliation" (October 2). Taken from *My Utmost for His Highest* by Oswald Chambers, edited by James Reimann, © 1992 by Oswald Chambers Publications Assn., Ltd., and used by permission of Discovery House Publishers, Grand Rapids, MI 49501. All rights reserved.

15. Silver, Larry B. *The Misunderstood Child: Understanding and Coping with Your Child's Learning Disability*, 4th Edition. New York: Three Rivers Press, 2006.

16. International Dyslexia Association. *www.interdys. org* "What is Dyslexia?" 17 August 2012. Used with permission. <http://www.interdys.org/FAQWhatIs. htm>

17. Silver, Larry B. *The Misunderstood Child: Understanding and Coping with Your Child's Learning Disability*, 4th Edition. New York: Three Rivers Press, 2006.

18. International Dyslexia Association. "Myths About Dyslexia." 17 August 2012. Used with permission. <http://www.interdys.org/MythsAboutDyslexia. htm>

19. Ibid.

20. Attention Deficit Disorder Association. "ADHD Fact Sheet." 17 August 2012. <http://www.add. org/?page=ADHD_Fact_Sheet>

21. Children and Adults with Attention Deficit / Hyperactivity Disorder. "What is ADHD?" 10 October 2012. <http://www.chadd.org/AM/ Template.cfm?Section=Understanding>

22. International Dyslexia Association. "Are Attention Deficit Disorder (ADD) and Attention Deficit Hyperactive Disorder (ADHD) Learning

Disabilities?" 17 August 2012. Used with permission.
<http://www.interdys.org/FAQAreADDand%20
ADHD.htm>

23. Attention Deficit Disorder Association. "ADHD
Fact Sheet." 17 August 2012. <http://www.add.
org/?page=ADHD_Fact_Sheet>

24. Family Vision Care. "Can a Dyslexic Be Successful
in a Career?" 1 October 2012. Used with permission of Dr. Sally Fife. <www.drsallyfife.com/
questions-about-dyslexia/>

25. Chambers, Oswald. "Christ-Awareness." (August
20th). Taken from *My Utmost for His Highest* by
Oswald Chambers, edited by James Reimann, © 1992
by Oswald Chambers Publications Assn., Ltd., and
used by permission of Discovery House Publishers,
Grand Rapids, MI 49501. All rights reserved.

26. Chambers, Oswald. "Spiritual Dejection" (February
7th). Taken from *My Utmost for His Highest* by
Oswald Chambers, edited by James Reimann, © 1992
by Oswald Chambers Publications Assn., Ltd., and
used by permission of Discovery House Publishers,
Grand Rapids, MI 49501. All rights reserved.

27. Chambers, Oswald. "Prayer: Battle in the Secret
Place" (August 23rd). Taken from *My Utmost for*

His Highest by Oswald Chambers, edited by James Reimann, © 1992 by Oswald Chambers Publications Assn., Ltd., and used by permission of Discovery House Publishers, Grand Rapids, MI 49501. All rights reserved.

28. Roberts, Frances J. "Ye Shall Not Be Earthbound." *Come Away My Beloved*. Uhrichsville, OH: Barbour Publishing, Inc., 1973. Page 60. Used with permission of Barbour Publishing, Inc.

29. Roberts, Frances J. "Rain." *Come Away My Beloved*. Uhrichsville, OH: Barbour Publishing, Inc., 1973. Page 98. Used with permission of Barbour Publishing, Inc.

30. Roberts, Frances J. "The Mind of God." *Come Away My Beloved*. Uhrichsville, OH: Barbour Publishing, Inc., 1973. Page 153. Used with permission of Barbour Publishing, Inc.

31. Roberts, Frances J. "Look Not Back." *Come Away My Beloved*. Uhrichsville, OH: Barbour Publishing, Inc., 1973. Page 110. Used with permission of Barbour Publishing, Inc.

32. Roberts, Frances J. "The Call of Love." *Come Away My Beloved*. Uhrichsville, OH: Barbour Publishing, Inc., 1973. Page 13. Used with permission of Barbour Publishing, Inc.

33. Roberts, Frances J. "Faith and Action." *Come Away My Beloved*. Uhrichsville, OH: Barbour Publishing, Inc., 1973. Page 15. Used with permission of Barbour Publishing, Inc.

34. Roberts, Frances J. "Ye Cannot Weary My Love." *Come Away My Beloved*. Uhrichville, OH: Barbour Publishing, Inc., 1973. Page 63. Used with permission of Barbour Publishing, Inc.

35. Roberts, Frances J. "Check Thy Course." *Come Away My Beloved*. Uhrichsville, OH: Barbour Publishing, Inc., 1973. Page 79. Used with permission of Barbour Publishing, Inc.

36. Roberts, Frances J. "The Healing Power of Joy." *Come Away My Beloved*. Uhrichsville, OH: Barbour Publishing, Inc., 1973. Page 33. Used with permission of Barbour Publishing, Inc.

CPSIA information can be obtained at www.ICGtesting.com
Printed in the USA
BVOW02s0519150514

353550BV00002BA/76/P

9 781624 197475